the Idler

ISSUE 39 | SPRING 2007

1 3 5 7 9 10 8 6 4 2

Published in 2007 by Ebury Press, an imprint of Ebury Publishing

Ebury Publishing is a division of the Random House Group

The Idler, Issue 39
© Copyright Idle Limited, 2007

The Random House Group Limited Reg. No. 954009

Addresses for companies within the Random House Group can be found at
www.randomhouse.co.uk

A CIP catalogue record for this book is available from the British Library

The Random House Group Limited makes every effort to ensure that the
papers used in our books are made from trees that have been legally sourced
from well-managed and credibly certified forests. Our paper procurement
policy can be found on www.randomhouse.co.uk

Cover illustration by Hannah Dyson
Typeset by Chloë King
Printed and bound by Firmengruppe APPL, aprinta druck, Wemding, Germany

ISBN 9780091916503

The views expressed by the contributors do not necessarily
reflect those of the editors

Where copyright material has been used we have attempted to trace copyright
holders. Any omissions can be rectified in future issues

Editor: Tom Hodgkinson   Art Director: Chloë King
Deputy Editor: Dan Kieran   Creative Director Emeritus: Gavin Pretor-Pinney
Editor at Large: Matthew De Abaitua
Literary Editor: Tony White   Sports Editor: John Moore
Music Editor: Will Hodgkinson   Motoring Editor: Fanny Johnstone
Contributing Editors: Greg Rowland, Ian Vince, Clare Pollard

WHAT IS THE IDLER?

THE IDLER IS A MAGAZINE
THAT CELEBRATES FREEDOM,
FUN AND THE FINE ART OF
DOING NOTHING.

WE BELIEVE THAT IDLENESS
IS UNJUSTLY CRITICIZED IN
MODERN SOCIETY WHEN IT IS,
IN FACT, A VITAL COMPONENT
OF A HAPPY LIFE.

WE WANT TO COMFORT
AND INSPIRE YOU WITH
UPLIFTING PHILOSOPHY,
SATIRE AND REFLECTION, AS
WELL AS GIVING PRACTICAL
INFORMATION TO HELP IN THE
QUEST FOR THE IDLE LIFE.

WHATEVER YOU DO, TAKE PRIDE.

THE ORIGINAL OFFENCE, P100

CONTENTS

THE IDLER *Issue 39, Spring 2007*

PROTEST AT G8 BY IMMO KLINK

CONTENTS

THE IDLER *Issue 39,*
Spring 2007

EDITOR'S LETTER

ANYTHING THAT attacks you, makes you stronger. It validates you. It makes you feel alive. You have been noticed. Hate is a form of love. Resentment a form of dependence.

When surveying the current state of the world, and the very many protests that have been launched on the prevailing order, one can't help concluding that physical protest, as an agent of positive change, is singularly ineffectual. Indeed, it may even have precisely the opposite effect to the one intended. Just as the cocaine dealer's best friend is the tabloid press for constantly promoting his product by salaciously and pruriently attacking it in their pages, so the anti-government protestor or anti-corporate protestor may in fact be their stated enemy's most effective ally. Take for example, talk of an oil crisis. If there is an oil crisis, in other words, if it is widely believed that oil supplies are running low, then clearly that is great news for the peddlers of oil, since by the laws of supply and demand, the fear of a crisis makes it easy for them to manipulate the price. So the oil-whingeing fraternity becomes its own arch-enemy's unpaid sales force. In the case of governments, a march along the Strand will merely serve to boost their self-importance. And when corporations are under attack, it gives their PR agents the opportunity to assume victim status. Finally, also, the "something must be done" school of political protest misses a fundamental truth: when too much "doing" is the problem, can more "doing" be a solution?

A studied neglect, an amused disenchantment, a spirited disengagement, a staying in bed: these may be far more subversive tools than banners, guns or petitions. Rather than trying to destroy our neighbour's castle, we ignore it and build one of our own. Or simply slip away into the woods.

Tom Hodgkinson
tom@idler.co.uk

IDLER CONTRIBUTORS

Who are the Idlers?

ALBERT COSSERY is a writer living in Paris

JEAN-PAUL BERTHOIN is a London-based photographer. You can see his work at www.berthoin.com

PETE BROWN is a beer expert and author or Two Sheets To The Wind: One Man's Quest for the Meaning of Beer (Macmillan)

CHRISTIAN BRETT is an artist and typesetter. www.bracketpress.com

ED CUMMING is a bright young thing

PAUL DAVIS works too hard and doesn't really want to any more

NICKY DEELEY quit her day job to make robotic animals and design a nightclub interior in Madrid and someone recently gave her an autoharp. www.squidbunny.net

CHLOE DEWE MATHEWS is soon to tour the world as The Human Tamborine

BILL DRUMMOND'S latest projects can be seen at www.penkiln-burn.com

ABIGAIL FALLIS trained at Camberwell College of Art. She is a sculptor and maker who uses her art to express her feelings about excessive consumption and environmental issues

MIREILLE FAUCHON is a printmaker and illustrator influenced by folk tales and local legends. Mireillefau@hotmail.com

RJ GHORBANI is an Anglo-Iranian misfit dedicated to fighting the forces of bureaucracy

JAY GRIFFITHS is the author of Pip Pip: A Sideways Look At Time and her new book is called Wild: An Elemental Journey (Hamish Hamilton)

PAUL HAMILTON is co-editor of How Very Interesting: Peter Cook's Universe And All That Surrounds It, published by Snowbooks, and drummist for Reticents and for Idle Tommy's City Slackers, or whatever the Idler's house ukulele band are called. No, he doesn't have a fucking mobile.

GEORGIA HARRISON draws with peculiar humour. With compliments email georgia.harrison@rca.ac.uk

MISHKA HENNER is one half of Commoneye. www.lightstalkers.com/mishkahenner

SANDRA HOWGATE lives in East London and likes to take long walks

TONY HUSBAND is cartoonist. His World's Worst Jokes is published by Ebury

HENRY JEFFREYS works for an eminent firm of publishers and runs the Gentleman's Breakfast Club

FANNY JOHNSTONE is our motoring editor

FUMIE KAMIJO sells freaky handmade dolls at the Sunday Up Market and from www.mybobbydazzler.com. Email fumie. kamijo@rca.ac.uk.

DAN KIERAN'S new book, I Fought The Law (Bantam Press) is out now, and he will be coming to a town near you in a milk float very soon

CHLOË KING likes the look of things. www.chloeking.co.uk

IMMO KLINK'S website is at www. immoklink.com

PETE LOVEDAY is the creator of Russell comics

MARK MANNING is not really a sex god from outer space

CORINNE MAIER is the author of Bonjours Paresse and has finally quit the day job

MATT MORDEN is author of the Morden Haiku blog at www.mordenhaikupoetry. blogspot.com and Associate Editor of Snapshots haiku magazine.

JOHN NICHOLSON is a hairy historian who has worked with Rioky Gervais, Graham Norton and Ant and Dec

ROB NICOL has a website, it's www.robert-nicol.co.uk

MARCUS O'DAIR is a freelance writer

JUSTIN POLLARD is the author of three books: *Alfred The Great*, *Seven Ages of Britain* and *The Rise and Fall of Alexandria*

JONATHAN PUGH draws cartoons for *The Times* and others

ANTHONY REYNOLDS is a musician. His latest release is *The Ponies* EP. www.anthonyreynolds.net

ROS RICHARDS is an illustrator currently studying at the RCA

PENNY RIMBAUD has disengaged. www.onoffyesno.com

GREG ROWLAND is a semiotic analyst

LA ROWLAND works in academia

JOCK SCOT now potters in Tufnell Park

BOB AND ROBERTA SMITH is the adopted persona of the artist Patrick Brill

HUGO TIMM is Brazilian and has been living in London since August 2006. hugotimm@gmail.com

ROBERT TWIGGER is the author of many books, including *Angry White Pyjamas* and *Big Snake*. See more at www.roberttwigger.com

JOANNA WALSH is otherwise known as Walshworks, and can be found at www.baduade.typepad.com or www.eastwing.co.uk

ANKE WECKMANN grew up in Germany, and came to London in 2001. She loves spring, elderflower cordial, stripey socks and Harriet the Spy. She also eats a lot of potatoes. www.Linotte.net

TONY WHITE is the *Idler*'s literary editor. His most recent book is the non-fiction work *Another Fool in the Balkans*.

ROBERT WRINGHAM is a freelance writer

GED WELLS did the *Idler* snail and he edits Trisikle skateboard magazine

APOLOGIES TO PHOTOGRAPHERS NICOLA EVANS AND DESIREE PFEIFFER, WHO TOOK OUR UKULELE GIRL PIC AND PHOTO OF MATTHEW REYNOLDS IN THE LAST ISSUE, AND WERE SCANDALOUSLY MISSED OUT FROM THE CONTRIBUTORS' SECTION

CLOCKWISE FROM TOP LEFT: CHLOË KING, MIREILLE FAUCHON, ANKE WECKMANN, NICKY DEELEY, HUGO TIMM, GEORGIA HARRISON

NOTES FROM THE COUCH

THE IDLER'S DIARY

TO BRUNSWICK in Germany for Faulheit, a symposium devoted entirely to idleness, organised by the University of Art there. Editor Tom was invited to speak and he joined five others for a day long programme of talks. Among the speakers were Eberhaud Straub, author of a recent book in Germany on the subject, and Alia Lira Hartman, a Mexican journalist now living in Germany. Alia's talk centred on the cultural differences between Germany and Mexico and in particular, their different attitudes to work and time. In Germany, she said, people ask you to dinner four weeks in advance, unthinkable in Mexico. Furthermore, she said that work and leisure were far more intertwined in Mexico, to the extent where people don't feel they need annual holidays to recover from work. The religious calender has umpteen festivals all year round. The symposium was also attended by a large number of art students, both from the college in Brunswick and from the University of Art and Design in Budapest. It appears that in each case, the institutions have received grants for idling: part of the project involves a month-long trip for each student to travel around and talk to people about their attitudes to work. They will then go home and produce work based on their researches. State-funded idling: it's got to be good. Next issue we will run some of the results of this fantastic project.

WE WERE ALSO able to visit Berlin on this trip, and the city seems to be going through a fascinating stage right now. It is filled with artists, who have been attracted there by the low cost of living. Maybe it's something to do with the fact that there is no financial district in Berlin, but for some reason the property prices are low, rents are low and the place is filled with cafés and bars. The ethic is distinctly unmaterialistic and the artists seem to be abe to combine family life with work seamlessly. There are plenty of young Dads wandering round with Baby Bjorns, swapping stories of infant sleep patterns. Worth checking out for those who are exploring alternatives to British metropolitan living.

TO MR B'S READING EMPORIUM, a proper, independent bookshop in Bath, where editor Tom gave a talk on freedom and idleness. The audience consisted of a varied selection of free spirits: there was a man who did long distance lorry-driving for two days a week, giving him five days off, and another chap who said he'd resolutely stuck to the bottom ranks of the civil service in order to give him a pleasant job with plenty of energy left over for other activities. It's good to see the ranks of the idlers swelling, and we're always interested in readers' accounts of how they have created their own lives.

IDLER'S DIARY CONTINUED

IDLER EDITORS Dan Kieran and Ian Vince are embarking on an odyssey this summer with their friend Prasanth Visweswarian to celebrate the art of slow travel for a book and Radio Four programme called *Three Men In a Float*. They will set out from the most easterly point in Britain, Lowestoft, and drive to the most westerly point, Lands End, with a maximum speed of fifteen miles per hour. However, every night the milkfloat will need to be charged by plugging into the electricity supplies of generous members of the public. So if you live anywhere on or near the line across the map below and you'd like to volunteer the nocturnal use of your power supply and put Dan, Ian and Prasanth up for the night then please email dan@idler.co.uk. Our brave adventurers are also looking for interesting places to visit and people to interview along the way, so if you'd like to suggest a particularly excellent pub/castle/forest/park bench/milkman/haunted house/caravan site/view/cafe/brewery etc that Dan, Ian and Prasanth should call upon on their journey then please get in touch.

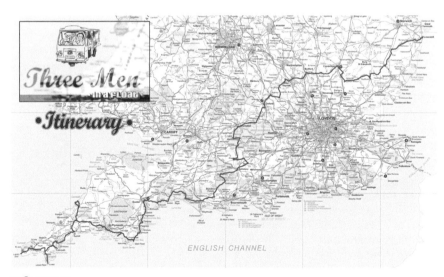

"MALCOLM'S ALWAYS BEEN AN ARMCHAIR PROTESTER"

by Jonathan Pugh

READERS' LETTERS

DEAR IDLER,

In 2002 my partner and I chucked in our crap jobs. We were within months of our fortieth birthdays. We had divorced from respective long-standing marriages the previous year and neither of us had dependent children. Together we bought a near-derelict "two up two down" Victorian terraced house in the Midlands for under £40k. We took a year off from our "careers" to renovate that house, yet on completion of the project we realised that neither of us could face a further 25 year sentence of credit cards, possessions and tedium. We've never had salaried jobs since then.

During our "sabbatical" we had started house-sitting for wealthier friends and relatives. We looked after their dogs, cats and houses whilst they took well deserved holidays. One day we just decided to try house sitting full-time. The mathematics weren't difficult; fund the whole deal with a re-mortgage, let the house to tenants to cover the payments, then buy a beefy tow-car and caravan to live in between house sits. Sorted. Oh, what about earning enough money for the essentials; beer, kebabs, wine, cider, vodka, gin, diesel, clothes and stuff? That's the difficult part.

We wanted everything totally above board, so we set up a bona-fide limited company, of which we're both PAYE employees, but we never earn enough money to pay tax. Everything's properly invoiced and there's nothing done for cash. The tricks are low overheads, transportable skills and savvy use of information technology. The low overheads are achieved by living in other peoples' houses at their expense. We don't have to pay a mortgage, we have no council tax, no utility bills, no gym fees, no commuting costs, nor any of those golden handcuffs which manacle regular citizens.

Between us, as well as industrially cleaning our clients' houses, and keeping their pets happy and healthy; we can also build basic websites, drive HGV's (if there is an employment agency nearby), paint and decorate, clear and landscape gardens, tile bathrooms and other odd-jobs. We've even swept someone's chimney as part of a deal. Accordingly, sometimes we can charge money for house sitting, sometimes not. It depends on the clients' needs and their closeness to their wallets.

We often house sit around Europe for UK expats with large properties. I'm typing this from a closed-for-winter hotel 3000 ft up in the French Pyrenees, in front of the crackling wood burner with the dog and two cats in our charge. The view from my 'office' window is stunning. We've been here since November, and snowed in for the last ten days. Thanks to the internet I can just, but only just, find enough design work to keep us in bread, cheese and wine. In my old life I worked in a windowless, fluorescent-lit basement for eight years at one stretch.

As a cyber-itinerant I always carry a Mac laptop and a 3G mobile phone that acts as an emergency modem if there's no ADSL signal. We obtain all our house sit assignments from our website, so we can't afford to miss just one e-mail message. An I-pod carries our CD collection and our life is permanently crammed into our old estate-car.

Being intentionally homeless can be tough sometimes. During the winter it's

Write to us at:
The Idler, P. O. Box 280, Barnstaple, EX31 4WX

too cold to live in the caravan between house sits in the UK, so if stuck we head down to the Spanish Costas, where the retired expats sometimes need odd jobs done in return for caravan space. We can't profess to be entirely idle, but we usually work when we need to, and usually from the nicer parts of the world.

The House-sitters

DEAR IDLER,

Society and inherent ethics try to mould and cajole us into numerous "ways of life" that given the choice we'd all spurn. These are typified in the endlessly depressing truisms that we are fooled into thinking are acceptable: "all good things must come to an end", "what goes up must come down", "you can have too much of a good thing" etc. Fortunately, publications such as *The Idler* rebuff these "ideals" and try to denounce the expectation of disappointment that is intrinsic in British society. However, society has won one battle in the war against professionalism. It's a battle that I intend to fight 'til the death.

The much-maligned Sunday. The day of rest. The day of indolence and the endangered lie-in. Our overworked, overtired, spent, money chasing population...well, they hate it. The majority of people you ask will say they can't stand Sundays. "There's nothing to do," they'll say. Employers have tricked a plenitude of us into thinking that the only day of the week when work stops, when businesses shut, when working hours are slashed is a boring day. A day of waste. Whereas in reality, Sunday isn't a day of waste at all - it's the best of all the seven days. There is no other day of the week when something as

seemingly trivial as sitting in the garden all afternoon would be deemed acceptable. There'd be "things to do" on a Saturday afternoon. Equally, reading the paper in bed is only appropriate on the day of lethargy and positive languor. Sunday idling is twisted by the powerful to seem boring. A common complaint is "there's nothing on the TV." But when else is there something worth watching at two in the afternoon? "There's nowhere to go." But why go somewhere when you involuntarily lumber somewhere five days a week?

The thing is that British people don't know how to deal with time to themselves. We'll look forward to a holiday for four months, but we're "ready for home" after two weeks. School children are granted six weeks to amble wherever they choose every year—after three they can't wait to get back to school. Sundays are so incongruous in our clustered, sweating, rushed lives that we find ourselves dismissing the idyllic nature of the day as boring. What a sorry state of affairs.

Appreciating Sundays just for their lethargic atmosphere would be the ideal starting place for removing some of the clutter from the inextricable maze of plans and deadlines that engulf us these days. Don't get me started on Monday mornings.

Sunday Man

DEAR IDLER,

Up until two years ago I had spent 25 years in the rat race doing stressful and very physical construction work. Life was about hard labour, pressure to get houses completed for the market, and then spending my high wages usually on alcohol to numb the stress, and other things

READERS' LETTERS CONTINUED

that I never needed. As time went on my general health deteriorated and I found myself having to take time off of work. It was during this time of enforced idling that I got a glimpse of how a new way of living could benefit me in many aspects of my life. This was also the time when I read *How to be Idle* and this book touched a chord in me and engendered a desire to follow my real passions. Now I only work part-time, (20 hrs per week). I now enjoy my work helping people with learning difficulties to play instruments and express themselves through music. I am doing things I never seemed to have time to do while I was lost in the cycle of earn and spend. I'm now the champion of my local pitch and putt nine hole golf course, I go for strolls along the canal, I reflect more and write songs and poems, I read for pleasure and inspiration and I spend a lot of time reclining on my couch in a state of suspended bliss. My health will never be perfect, but it has improved and this is all because I chose living over working. There is of course the issue of having less money. What I have found is that you cut your cloth to suit your circumstances. When I was earning seven hundred pounds a week my account was always just slightly in profit, now its just the same. I've just learned to spend less and don't buy crap things I don't need. As a result life is less cluttered and I am freed from most responsiblity and angst.
Thanks Tom, for your inspiration,
Ian Duncan
Falkirk.

DEAR IDLER,

On my way into Iraq, I skived *How to be Idle*, book off the U.S. Army. The hardcover was among several donated books sitting in a dilapidated tent in an isolated army camp in the middle of a desolate stretch of Kuwaiti desert.

We had stopped in Kuwait to conduct some remedial training, but our primary mission was to learn how to fully enjoy the hellish 140 degree sun. There we learned that to survive our miserable stint in Iraq we would have to 1) Become skilled at spotting roadside bombs, and 2) Become accustomed to long periods of doing absolutely nothing.

While your book has not been tremendous help with the former, it has been great aid in adapting to the mind-numbingly slow pace of the army. After reading your book, I find my sanity much improved.

To whoever it was that donated your book, I would like to extend my sincere appreciation for relieving me of my anxiety for inactivity. I will pass the book, along with my small collection of the *Idler*, to the poor bastard that replaces me.
Peace,
Joe Vincello, Captain, U.S. Air Force
Al Asad Air Base, Iraq

DEAR TOM,

I just wanted to mention how tattoos and our iPods have helped us to be free. Not being the world's most handsome guy (an understatement really!) I have really enjoyed adorning myself with 24 tattoos over the past 14 months. It was something I'd wanted to do for years, but had always been afraid to do, for all the reasons you cite, so I waited till I was nearly46! But it's pure body art and beauty for beauty's sake. My two tattoo artists (one in Canada, where we have family, and one locally here in Forest Gate) are fantastic

artists, and it's great to carry their work around on me all the time. My wife has one, and my sons (aged 21 and 19) both have a few too. We all have iPods too, and they allow us to listen to the music we like, without adverts every few minutes and without having to listen to inane news bulletins. Admittedly they have the potential to make us isolated and anti-social, but we have a rule never to listen to them in the company of others.

Lynne and I will be idling in France next week, a country that still values its culture, food, drink, art and literature over working and making money, but I make it my business to remind my French friends never to take these for granted, and to fight for their survival.

I shall be taking 'How to be Idle' with me,

as well as my newly-delivered first copy of 'The Idler', and am looking forward to reading them both. I loved the certificate that came with my first copy of 'The Idler' - thank you very much. I was sorry not to be able to join you all in Bethnal Green last week, but I hope there will be further occasions when I can do so. In the meantime, if ever you are passing through Forest Gate E7, please be assured of a warm welcome if you feel like dropping in. We tend to drink more wine than beer, but there's always French lager down in the shed for just such occasions if you prefer, and plenty of home cooking.

Many thanks once again for your inspiration, and keep up the good work.
Best wishes,
Mike Richardson.

SKIVERS AND
HEROES AND VILLAINS

MR HUDSON AND THE LIBRARY

A classy diverse band lead by the trilby-wearing Ben Hudson, whose tailoring bears witness to a youth well-spent reading *The Chap* and *The Idler*. Even appearing on Jools Holland's honky-tonk piano show did not dull their lustre. "Why must I always play the clown?" sings Mr Hudson. We know exactly how that feels.

F SCOTT FITZGERALD

The novels of the booze-soaked laureate of the Great American Failure consider all the crucial Idler themes: what are the consequences of living only for the present moment? How can a refined gentleman possibly sully himself with tedious labour? And in both *Tender Is The Night* and *The Beautiful And Damned*, the perils to an idle sod of taking on a high maintenance missus.

COMMUTING

Listen, by the time you are 35, you'll be glad of the time to yourself.

STRIVERS
OF THE IDLE UNIVERSE

SPORTS DAY
You never won a race. Your children never win a race. And all around competitive parents are yabbering on: "My boy should have won, but the bastards gave him the heaviest sack!"

THE PLAN
"I've pinned a chart on the fridge that sets out my goals. I will achieve them all by the time I am thirty! What do you think of that?" "Does it include the goal of being less of a twat?"

VEGAS
The neon. The air-conditioning. The endless slot machines. One city that single-handedly wipes out all savings on carbon emissions made by the British middle class.

READING NEWSPAPERS
Like washing your face in dirty water.

I READ THE NEWS TODAY, OH FUCK

THE SOCIAL SCRUTINY GUIDE TO HOME SECURITY

As *Crimewatch*'s Nick Ross will almost certainly tell you, a lot of people make a lot of money out of scaring old people, so don't fall into the trap. Secure your home against midnight stranglers, prowling wolves and organ-transplant thieves and, please, please, don't have nightmares.

Cut down on heating bills
And improve security by not removing the front wall of your home.

Do not let strangers in
It's no coincidence that *stranger* and *strangler* are almost spelled the same way.

Cooking smells
Most burglars are familiar with the technique of using timers to turn lights on and off. By using the oven timer to bake cakes through the night and playing a never-ending tape loop of *The Archers* theme tune, you can disorientate and deter burglars by making them believe it is actually the middle of the day.

Improve your dog
Increase its fierceness by dressing it in a slashed-up tartan dog blanket. Lower the frequency of its adenoidal yap by fitting a baritone bark enhancer, otherwise known as a sub-woofer.

A Department of Social Scrutiny Infoganda Leaflet

Channelled by Ian Vince / www.socialscrutiny.org

The Shed

If you need to summon help in the event of a burglary, you can usually find the gentleman of the house in here, fiddling with a broken toaster.

The Lawn

Fill lawn sprinklers with undiluted hydrochloric acid, and wire up to a motion detector to instantly dissolve burglars, next door's cat and any tree branches that haplessly stray over the boundary.

The Garage

Secure your garage by filling it to the top with soil.

Be alarmed

Burglars are alarmed by burglar alarms, but many have learnt how to disconnect them so, if you have one fitted, make sure you secure it by fitting a further burglar alarm to its cover, securing the additonal alarm by wiring it to the first.

IAN VINCE

THE JOYS OF IMPERFECTION

Matt Morden on wabi sabi, the Japanese art of the rustic and incomplete

While clearing out my parents' shed recently, I came across an old hoe. My dad had bought it in a farm sale for a few pounds. The handle is worn, the blade rusty and chipped. It looks like it has done for thousands of weeds and spends every winter gathering cobwebs. It has a quality that cannot not be bought from B & Q. It is wabi sabi.

Wabi sabi is a Japanese concept that fits well with an idle lifestyle. Unlike its' better known cousin Feng Shui, it has nothing to do with the acquisition of wealth, fame or power. It is about a way of life based around noticing those every day moments often overshadowed in a buy now, pay later culture.

While wabi originally meant the loneliness of living in nature, remote from society, the origins of wabi sabi lay the Japanese tea ceremony of the Middle Ages. The throwing of tea parties by noblemen and military leaders was often used as a show of wealth using elaborate teapots and expensive gifts. However, the Zen monks who had brought the tea ceremony to Japan developed different wabi tea ceremonies. These were based around the natural elements used in making the tea and the simple raku pottery bowls used to serve it. Their emphasis was on the pleasure of drinking the tea and appreciation of the natural world around them.

The word sabi originated from Japanese poetry. It expresses the type of melancholia that you might feel looking back at your own footsteps on virgin snow, or sensing the first autumn chill on an August evening. Canadian wabi sabi author Richard R Powell describes this as the recognition that "nothing is perfect, nothing lasts and nothing is finished, but even so life is full of meaning." The whole term wabi sabi is a description of a simple way of life in which there is awareness of the significance of everyday moments and acceptance of the transience of life.

My own awareness of things wabi sabi began on the 4th March 1974, when my English teacher chose to discuss haiku with a class of Welsh twelve-year-olds. While this may have passed many of my classmates by, a haiku by a lesser known Japanese poet, Kikaku, struck a chord with me that has continued to resonate ever since.

> Bright the full moon shines
> on the matting of the floor
> shadows of the pines

Having spent many hours lying in bed watching the shadows of the pines on the floor, I knew what he meant. And while it would be many years until I wrote an even half-decent haiku myself, reading this set me off on a journey of discovery that, thanks to poets like Basho, Shiki and Jack Kerouac, continues to this day.

While the conventional view of haiku is that it is a three line poem with 17 syllables divided 5/7/5, it is the wabi sabi elements of the form that most interest me. Haiku offers an opportunity to put into words the acceptance of transience and the beauty of the imperfect, impermanent and incomplete. In a world where it's all too easy to overlook the pleasures of a cup of tea, a lettuce fresh from the garden or the sound of the midnight shipping forecast, I think that can only be a good thing.

Matt Morden is author of the Morden Haiku blog: www.mordenhaikupoetry.blogspot.com and Associate Editor of Snapshots *haiku magazine.*

ROSALIND RICHARDS

LAW, LIBERTY AND THE SEARCH FOR ALBION

In the introduction to his new book, Dan Kieran explains how he set out to break barmy old laws but uncovered a host of barmy new laws instead. He soon found himself fighting for common liberties

Voltaire once quipped, "I do not agree with what you have to say, but I'll defend to the death your right to say it." The use of a quotation from a Frenchman to define what it means to be British may offend some, but then that neatly sums up the contradictory nature of the British people. Sadly, today no one can claim that Voltaire's words speak for this country any more. On 1 August 2005, to the widespread shrugging of shoulders across the land, it became illegal to hold a spontaneous political demonstration outside the House of Commons. The nation's apathy towards losing the right to free speech at the seat of its government, something supposedly as intrinsic to this "green and pleasant land" as warm beer and Freddie Flintoff, posed the question what, if anything, does Britain actually stand for today?

Twenty miles from London, along the Thames, you will find a field opposite an island in the river. The field contains a monument erected by the American Bar Association. In the field next to it there is a memorial garden to John F. Kennedy to commemorate his role in the Civil Rights movement. Why on earth, you may imagine, are there American monuments in fields by the Thames? There are no other monuments. There is nothing to commemorate anything British. Perhaps an important figure in American history was born there? Nope. The site is far more important to the American people than that. On that unmarked island, in 1215, something was written down that over five hundred years later became the Fifth Amendment of the American Bill of Rights. "No freeman shall be taken, imprisoned... or in any other way destroyed... except by the lawful judgment of his peers, or by the law of the land. To no-one will we sell, to none will we deny or delay, right or justice." For Americans, this became, "No person shall... be deprived of life, liberty, or property, without due process of law." The original document was, of course, the Magna Carta.

Nearly eight hundred years ago King John was held to account by a group of rebel barons who demanded a charter of liberties to protect England from his unfair and erratic behaviour. That was when

PIC 1: ARTIST NEIL GOODWIN STANDS OUTSIDE DOWNING STREET

the principle of a power higher than the sovereign was established. That higher power was the rule of law. The Magna Carta has since been described as the most potent symbol of freedom under law in western civilization. It is something, you would imagine, that even our embarrassed nation would manage to be proud of. At the very least you'd think we might have one of those blue plaques down there somewhere. "Liberty under law started here," perhaps, nailed to a nearby tree. It would be nice to have something to commemorate the birth of British freedom, but there is nothing.

Today, Britain, and the Western world, hosts another dominant power that behaves pretty much as it likes and there seems little chance that it will be forced to adhere to a higher law. This dominant power is not even bound by any laws of basic morality. In fact, according to the American Bar Association[1] and the late Milton Friedman, one of the most influential economists of all time, it is actually illegal for a corporation to act altruistically or for the good of their community, country or, heaven forbid, the world.[2] A CEO who puts the interests of the community ahead of the company's shareholders could actually be sent to prison. You see, King John had nothing on the modern-day corporation.

If we all lived in a corporation rather than a country, then at least we would reap the benefits of this immoral logic. But unlike corporations, most societies consider basic morality to be something of value. The government, meanwhile, is doing all it can to help corporations turn us into consumers of Britain rather than citizens of it. So I thought I'd better go out

PIC 2: POLICE INFORM NEIL THAT HE IS BREAKING SECTION 132 OF THE SERIOUS AND ORGANISED CRIME AND POLICE ACT, 2005

and find the Britain of our dreams, sometimes known as Albion, so we can all go and live there instead. Which brings me to my book.

Originally the book was supposed to be a guide to some of the most absurd ancient legislation still on the statute book. I'd had this great idea to go round the country on a crime spree breaking as many silly old laws as I could find, for your amusement. There are hundreds of these ridiculous laws still in force in Britain. For example, to this day it is illegal to flag down a London taxi if you have the plague. In Chester you can't shoot a Welshman with a bow and arrow before midnight, but you can after midnight. It's also against the law to beat a carpet in the Metropolitan Police District. Neither can you carry a sack of soot along a path in a place called Congleton, and it is still unlawful

to get within a few hundred yards of the Queen without wearing socks. The list goes on and on. However, in the process of researching these laws I couldn't help noticing another glut of legislation that seemed even more ludicrous. Great, you may think, but no. You see, there was one problem. Most of our silly laws have trickled onto the statute book over centuries, but this particular set had all come from our current government. And when you meet a man who got arrested after eating a cake with "Freedom of Speech" written on it in icing, and someone else who has a criminal record for holding a banner made of fridge packing in Parliament Square that had "Freedom of Speech" written on it in biro, the idea of breaking the Adulteration of Tea Act of 1776 starts to seem a little frivolous. Of course, once I started lifting up this legal concrete slab

PIC 3: NEIL IS ARRESTED. PICTURES BY RACHEL POULTON

in the garden of England all sorts of other creepy crawlies emerged that cast doubt on the health of the nation. So this book became, quite by coincidence, a very different thing entirely.

Of course, on paper Britain is doing rather well for itself. We have enjoyed unparalleled economic prosperity since Labour came to power. There are more billionaires in the UK today than ever before, there are more shiny things to spend our money on than you could possibly imagine, and, despite widely being portrayed as America's lapdog, we do appear to have some standing in the world at large. But who else lives in Britain apart from all the high-flyers, over-achievers and entrepreneurs who have helped this great land to secure membership of the G8, the club for the most economically powerful nations on earth? How does Britain seem to eve-rybody else who lives here? You know, the other ones. You and me. Those of us floundering in the highest levels of debt in Europe; the ones afraid of poverty in retirement; the ones being forced to work forty-plus hours a week with only four weeks off a year; the ones terrified of violent crime, of their children being adversely affected by the MMR jab; the ones suffering from depression because they can't handle the stress of their jobs; the ones Carol Vorderman is hoping will consolidate their debt so she can keep her no doubt lucrative advertising contract; even those who aren't born yet hoping to live here one day too, the future generations who will be around when the icecaps start to melt and vast swathes of this country vanish under the ocean.

To find out, I went on a journey around Britain to meet some of the people still fighting for Albion among the uniform high streets, no-go estates, monochrome offices and shopping malls of corporate Britain. I found an unlikely selection of eccentrics to guide me on my journey who, incidentally, weren't fighting against the government or the corporations profiting from this land; they were fighting *for* something instead, which is a much more powerful incentive. On one level they were simply fighting for themselves and their communities; on another they were fighting for every one of us hoping to enjoy Britain's future. People like the pensioners who let off stink bombs to force an extension to a public inquiry. The hairy history expert who got paid to have custard pies thrown at his beard by Ant and Dec. The man who dresses like Chaplin's tramp and keeps getting arrested outside Downing Street because we no longer have the right to remain silent either. The world-famous fisherman with a penchant for firing home-made rockets into space. The man who enjoys howling like a wolf in his back garden. The Robin Hood of the squatting world who gets into empty buildings and hands the keys over to homeless people who can't afford anywhere to live. The woman living on the roof of a bus station in Derby. An activist who organizes picketing campaigns outside the homes of drug dealers. The ex-MI5 agent now reduced to peddling conspiracy theories to complete strangers about 9/11. Along with encouragement from Billy Childish (one of Kurt Cobain's favourite musicians), Gavin Hills, Arthur Pendragon, George Orwell and William Blake. And Britain needs these people.

It needs them all because things are getting a bit Monty Python down in Albion. From the towns we live in to the countryside itself, the cult of overwork and over-consumption is spreading like a disease, bringing with it a greater dependence on anti-depressants, huge numbers of stress-related health problems and tightening us all in an ever-growing grip of fear. Fear of violent crime, fear of poverty in retirement, fear of global warming and, of course, the greatest of them all: the fear of terrorism. Today, the wonder of Albion, if it ever existed, certainly seems to have been obliterated by Britain plc. And it's not just an ideological shift being discussed over cigars and whisky by the political fraternity, it's a reality that's changing every aspect of our daily lives. As you'll discover, if you read my book, anyone who actually wants to behave like a citizen of this country, rather than just a consumer of it, quickly finds themselves on the wrong side of the law . 🐌

[1] "While allowing directors to give consideration to the interests of others, [the law] compel[s] them to find some reasonable relationship to the long-term interests of shareholders when so doing." *American Bar Association, Committee on Corporate Laws, "Other constituencies Statutes: Potential for confusion," The Business Lawyer 45 (1990): 2261, as cited in G. Smith, "The Shareholder Primacy Norm".*
[2] "A corporation is the property of its stockholders... Its interests are the interests of its stockholders. Now, beyond that should it spend the stockholders' money for purposes which it regards as socially responsible but which it cannot connect to its bottom line? The answer I would say is no." *The Corporation by Joel Bakan, Free Press, 2004*

I Fought The Law by Dan Kieran (Bantam Press) is published on 7th May 2007.

REAL FIRES

A fire in the hearth offers umpteen opportunities for pleasurable pootling. First there is the enjoyable palaver of making and lighting the fire. There are the twigs to be found, the newspaper to be scrunched up, the kindling to be laid, or the firelighters to be lit if you are a modern type. Then the satisfying blaze as the paper and twigs go up. Following that the fire will settle down and need only the occasional poke and log thrown on top. And then you can indulge yourself in fireside staring, watching the dancing shapes that make up ever-changing fire. So much more romantic and creatively useful, not to say pleasurable, than the infernal radiator. In the traditional village house, the fire is in the centre of the room because it is all life that gathers round the fire, source of heat, light and delightful reveries. So much more fascinating than its urban counterpart, the television. 🐌

IN PRAISE OF THE CAFF

Forget organic pretension and embrace the caff, says Henry Jeffreys

In Britain we have a problem with breakfasts, in fact we have a problem with food in general and like a lot of problems in this country it boils down to class. I speak of the great divide between the caff and the café. In the caff you will be served enormous quantities of not very good quality food quickly and with no pretension or fuss. In the café, there may be a mission statement, there may be a picture of Nicaraguan peasants children dancing happily because their parents have got a good price for their coffee, there may well be a family tree showing the lineage of the pork products. This will all be a mask to hide the fact that they don't really know what they are doing. The service will be terrible, the sausages will be over-cooked and the eggs will be under-cooked. In places like this, I look at the quality of the ingredients and weep at the waste and weep at the bill too which normally tops £7 for a full English. Complaining is pointless because all the staff are part-time and most of them are as hungover as the clientele.

What they lack is discipline!

Back at the caff, a stern patriarch (probably called Nico and of Greek Cypriot origin), will be conducting his kitchen in a symphony of steam and hissing fat. Your food will arrive miraculously quickly and will be exactly how you ordered it. The problem comes when you start to think about where your food comes from. Those peculiar brown/grey bangers are fine for the lower orders who have never tasted better but once you have tried a proper sausage then you will not want to go back.

What's to be done? I would love to see a reality TV show where Nico is sent into one of these organic rip-off joints to put the fear of God into the pretty fey staff. That would make excellent television and probably a very good breakfast. Alternatively greasy spoon caffs could offer a better class of sausage and bacon alongside the traditional tat. In a masterstroke the decline of the caff would be halted. You would have the best of both worlds, the caff and the café. The middle class would eat roughly the same food on the same premises as the working class. England would be one nation for the first time since the Norman conquest.

ROB NICHOL

DORSET CEREALS
COMPETITION

Your chance to win books and cereal!

The people at Dorset Cereals, makers of tasty cereals, are putting spring well and truly in their step and taking the task of idling very seriously. Dorset Cereals has teamed up with the Cloud Appreciation Society to leisurely appreciate the simple pleasures in life. As the weather begins to brighten, we'll be mastering the noble art of idling and taking in the wonder of our spectacular skies.

Dorset Cereals is giving 20 lucky *Idler* readers the chance to win a copy of the new paperback edition of the best-selling *Cloudspotter's Guide* by Gavin Pretor-Pinney and a yummy selection of Dorset Cereals. Enjoy a scrumptious Dorset Cereals breakfast as the perfect start to a wonderful day ahead – doing whatever you love to do best!

The Dorset Cereals range of tasty cereals includes classic **Simply Delicious Muesli,** the crunchy blend of **Really Nutty Muesli, Super High Fibre** with whole roasted hazelnuts or the highly nutritious **Fruit, Nuts & Seeds** – now also available as an **Organic** recipe. If you like something a little fruitier, you'll love **Super Cranberry, Cherry & Almonds**, combining jumbo Chilean flame raisins and sultanas with the tangy mix of cherries and cranberries – or **Berries & Cherries** with 50% premium fruit including juicy raspberries, blackcurrants, cranberries, blueberries and cherries.

For a more warming start to the day, try Dorset Cereals Fruity Porridges: **Apple & Raisin**, **Fruit & Nut** and **Mixed Berries**.

All the recipes use the finest combination of delicious fruits, nuts and seeds, which are blended using a special process that means there's less dust in each pack. You can find the range, priced from £1.99, in all major supermarkets, as well as delicatessen, convenience stores and health food shops nationwide.

For more information, please visit the website: www.dorsetcereals.co.uk.

TO ENTER:

To claim your free copy of the new paperback edition of The Cloudspotter's Guide, simply write the answer to the following question on postcard:
Dorset Cereals are makers of: a) milk? b) tasty cereals? c) spoons?
Send it with your name and address to: Idler Comp, Wild Card, Brettenham House, 1 Lancaster Place, London WC2E 7EN. Competition entries must be received by October 1st.

SATIRICAL SCRAPBOOK

Bob and Roberta Smith

In this series of throwaway drawings, the artist Bob and Roberta Smith recycles images torn from glossy news magazines, adapting and defacing them with scribbled slogans on a political or eco-activist theme. The butterfly, we assume, is saying 'See ya!' on behalf of an entire genus at risk of extinction. Others, such as 'Tony Blair is a wanker', are more straightforward.

For more information about Bob and Roberta Smith's work see http://home. clara.net/sg/bob_and_ roberta_smith/ or listen to the Bob and Roberta Smith radio show, Make Your Own Damn Music, on Resonance 104.4 FM every Tuesday at 9.00 PM, or via the webstream on www. resonancefm.com

THE WIT AND WISDOM OF

CAPTAIN BEEFHEART

Paul Hamilton selects choice quips from the clamlike genius

CAPTAIN BEEFHEART WITH FRANK ZAPPA, 1969

The playwright Harold Pinter opined that up to seventeen different meanings could be read into his characters' dialogue, although quite what he meant by that is open to debate. Captain Beefheart—Don Van Vliet, however, being the name on his bus pass—relished and explored the possibilities of word-play with childlike enthusiasm both in his songs and in life. What, for instance, did he mean when he stated in a 1993 telephone interview that he was "Happy as a clam"? On the surface it's a funny, oddball statement, redolent of his song titles ("When I See Mommy I Feel Like A Mummy", "A Carrot Is As Close As A Rabbit Gets To A Diamond"). Scratch it and various truths can be discerned: like a clam, Van Vliet has rarely been seen in public over the past two decades since he quit music to devote his days to painting. He has retreated from the material world to exist in a shell of his own making. There are rumours of debilitating, fading health, and in his last filmed appearance—in the Anton Corbijn short, "Some Yo-Yo Stuff"

(1994)—he looked perished and sounded short of breath, though not short of inspiration.

Captain Beefheart danced down a very singular path—deeply influential as a symbol of the possibilities of self-expression (John Peel, Simpsons' creator Matt Groening and ex-Pistol John Lydon—who namechecked a Beefheart instrumental, "Japan In A Dishpan", on the Sex Pistols' *New York*—are only three who cite him an inspiration), but never remotely so much as tickling the foot of the Musician Other Bands Want To Sound Like chart. To most ears, Beefheart sounds like a gout-afflicted meths-gargler accompanied by a drumkit being hurled down a staircase and guitars played by deaf octopuses. What sounds like cacophony is actually meticulously arranged, harmonically complex composition, borne out by the existence of live versions recorded years later with different line-ups of players that sound exactly like the original studio recordings. So rare it is for Beefheart to be heard on the airwaves that when an old track of his was played on a Saturday morning, an exultant Joe Strummer phoned the BBC. His yells of "I don't believe it! Captain Beefheart on Radio Two!" became a jingle (and, coincidentally, marked the first time in ages that Strummer appeared on daytime radio).

Here we celebrate the good Captain, with a beef in his heart about Man's relentless war against nature and harmony. The old fart was smart indeed!

WORLD RECLUSIVE:

The way I keep in touch with the world is very gingerly—because the world touches too hard. (1994)

SOCIAL INADEQUACY:

You have to excuse me, but I'm seven people away from myself at the moment, but I'm getting closer all the time. (Introducing himself to John Peel.)

AIRPLANE DESIGNS SIGNAL THE HUMANS' REJECTION OF THE NATURAL WORLD:

That was when everything got real pointed. Like the DC3 as opposed to the F104 or the Boeing. I mean, like the Sabre jet, emulating the shark as opposed to now they're emulating needles and things. (1972)

WRITING METHODS:

Q: Do you use a typewriter?

A: What type of writer do you mean? A flesh writer or a flesh writer with buttons? (1972)

THE LAUGHING GNOMIC NO. 1:

A psychiatrist is someone who wants to die in your next life.

ON HIS SONG "SAFE AS MILK" (1967):

I'll tell you what that meant: The mother's breast that's going to be unfit for the child because of Strontium 90, the hot juices of the breast. Everybody thought

CAPTAIN BEEFHEART PAINTING FOR THE BACK SLEEVE
OF SHINY BEAST (BAT CHAIN PULLER) LP, 1978

I meant acid, but I wouldn't talk about an aspirin at that length. I was inferring that the feeling that something is "safe as milk" can't be a feeling any more because milk isn't safe. (1972)

RACISM:

Everyone's coloured or you wouldn't be able to see them. (1980)

SEXISTENCE NO. 1:

[Architects] build all these red, male, blood, phallic buildings. You know what an architect is? A man who crawls up his own penis to pull up a shade and design all night. (1972)

TWO OLD SCHOOLFRIENDS DISTURBED AT 6AM:

Frank Zappa: That was an earthquake. Did you hear it?

Captain Beefheart: Yes, but it was so small that it made the people enormous. (1969)

MUSICAL HEROES:

A gander goose could be a hero, the way they blow their heart out for nothing like that. (1980)

FILM VILLAIN:

I don't like Walt Disney. He gave the wolf capital punishment. (1971)

REFUSAL TO ANALYSE THE SOURCES OF CREATION:

You don't want to get into the bullshit to find out what the bull ate.

THE LAUGHING GNOMIC NO.2:

There are forty people in the world and five of them are hamburgers.

THE SOLIPSISTIC MANIFESTO:

If you want to be a different fish you've got to jump out of the pool. (1980)

SEXISTENCE NO. 2:

I think it's important that there be some men who appreciate women for what they are—women. Not as some kind of extension of man. There's been a big ecological imbalance for years, what with women taking a backseat to men for so long. Their influence on life has been mutated and, because of it, the men have been getting into wars and screwing things up. My inspiration comes from appreciating women for what they are. (1972)

ANIMAL TESTING:

On my place I have lots of goats, horses, cows, cats, dogs. A lot of other animals eat here too—raccoons, coyotes, even a badger—gorgeous, tough, funny little animal. [Humans] learned karate from cats. The way they move their hands in karate is the same way cats move their tails when they encounter one another. (1972)

FIRST THOUGHT ABOUT A MONKEY:

Nice hairdo. (1994)

THE PAST SURE IS TENSE:

It makes me itch to think of myself as Captain Beefheart. I don't even have a boat. (1991)

AFTER U2'S SINGER OFFERS BEEFHEART THE SUPPORT SLOT OF AN EARLY 1990S TOUR:

Who is this *Bongo*?

THE LAUGHING GNOMIC NO.3:

The ocean takes all day to wave.

LIVING ART:

Q: What was the first picture you can remember painting, and how do you feel about it now?

A: It probably doesn't even remember me. (1994)

EASEL FOR YOU TO SAY:

Art is as close as you can get to perfection without being caught up in the wank. (1994)

GERMANE SENSE OF HUMOUR:

One joke I sure do agree with. It's a joke that the Chinese are killing tigers. They have a pussy problem! (1994). 🌀

CAPTAIN BEEFHEART 1969

MEMORANDA

Sir—

Here in North Devon we may not be the sharpest knives in the political drawer but, by God! we have a long tradition of Nimbyism, and the incomers have brought their own brand with them too, even if we don't always see eye to eye. What's more, many of us in the Countryside Alliance were there on the London march two years ago, when the police appeared to forget which side they were supposed to be on and brutally attacked decent rural persons of good Anglo-Saxon stock.

I realise the police must have the right to use strict physical measures against anarchist tree huggers, pinko strikers, Islamic traitors and other underclass scum, but I also understand why this lapse on the part of the forces of law and order should have left some bad feelings. However, I view with horror the proposal to erect a 350' high concrete 'Monument to the Unknown Protestor'. While this is infinitely preferable to a wind farm I cannot believe that Exmoor is an appropriate setting for 'Modern Art'. Besides, it could so easily fall into the wrong hands. I hasten to add I am not a philistine and own a fine collection of hunting prints.

Yrs. Etc.
'Confused' (ret.)

by Tony Husband

BILL AND ZED'S BAD ADVICE

WE'VE FUCKED UP OUR LIVES. NOW IT'S YOUR TURN

DEAR BILL AND ZED,

Nearly every night, in the wee hours, my dear partner will fidget in bed. His stirring rouses me and I wonder if I am about to get lucky, but instead of tending to his lady, he rises and sneaks off to the kitchen to seek goodies in the cupboards. He will usually break off some chunks of the chocolate I keep for special occasions and return to our bed. Whilst I feign sleep, he sucks and slurps said chocolate for the next ten minutes. It makes me angry and disappointed because it disturbs my sleep and disturbs his waistline. I require your suggestions to stop this filthy habit. Idlemother

ZED: What kind of wretched woman refers to herself as "his lady", keeps bars of chocolate for special occasions, lacks the tenacity to instigate carnal expression herself and finds her partner disgusting for merely eating said chocolate in bed?

Some fucked up, frigid, old horsehair minge bitch from the fifties, is what.

Listen you Idlemother miserable cunt, write to us when you've got something real to complain about, like when chocolate boy turns up wankered at four in the morning for instance, with a couple of his mates in tow, equally bladdered and lairy, demanding that you give them a free ride on your shitlocker.

Then perhaps we may grant you our sage counsel.

BILL: Although I tend to agree with Z there is something I would like to add —take up midnight gardening. As soon as the fidgeting starts, get out of bed, before he does go down stairs, put on an overcoat and Wellington boots and go out into the garden and start tending your vegetable plot. And if you don't have a garden get an allotment. There is always work to be done in a vegetable plot. The reward and returns you get from growing vegetables always outstrip those you get from the marital bed.

HEY B & Z,

My Gran is sixty seven years old and desperate to have IVF, thereby earning herself a place in the Guinness Book of Records as Europe's oldest mother. Trouble is, she needs a sperm donor and rings me every night begging for my love monkeys. I love my Gran very much but it just doesn't feel right. Please help me. Should I let the monkeys loose? Confused

ZED: Confused, dear boy, what kind of selfish, ungrateful little bastard grandson are you? Your poor old Gran, fast approaching the Alzheimer years, is obviously feeling lonely and in need of affection. Do the right thing. Get round there pronto and give the old dear a proper rigid seeing to, after all, she is your Gran.

Incest young man!

If it's good enough for the Hebrews and our handsome, good looking Royal family, it's good enough for you.

BILL: Of course there is another plan of action—kill her. It is an affront to the laws of nature all these women above the age of forty wanting to have children. Made worse when they know the chance of them having mongs is far greater by doing so. It is a well known medical fact that a woman's best child bearing years are between 16-24. All these so called professional women wanting to have a career before doing their duty has caused havoc enough with society already.

DEAR BILL AND ZED,

Last week my wife went to a hen party. There, the women played a game in which they had to stick a photograph of the groom's penis on a donkey. It was erect, and I wonder if his fiancé had taken the picture especially for the occasion. Anyway, when my wife was telling me this story she became quite wistful at the recollection of it. Is she about to go off the rails?
William Mooch

ZED: William, stout fellow, I'm afraid it's already too late to start worrying about wifey now. If she's going to hen parties on a regular basis her trolley careered off the track long ago.

Hen parties, as my former male stripper colleague Bill has informed me, are nothing more than an excuse for shatteringly drunk women to indulge in all manner of dripping, fellatory, analistic high jinks, male strippers wanking all over the place, spunking on shrieking, demented har-

ridans like there was no tomorrow, you name it, the works.

Pinning the bellend on the donkey was just the tip of an extremely mentally ill debauched iceberg, dear fellow.

Console yourself lad, with a trip to the nearest whorehouse.

Sauce for the gander, goose spunk and all that.

BILL: Sadly my days as a male stripper are well and truly behind me now. Although my erect member would initially cause squeals of delight when first exposed to the hen revellers, it was the after effects that caused me to reconsider my profession. If it wasn't the ripped sphincters needing instant A&E, it was the one that couldn't get enough, mistaking a night of fun and frolics as a declaration of life long love. There were also the jealous husbands and boyfriends who somehow thought it just to seek revenge on me because they could no longer impress their woman.

My advice to you is to set up in business as a male stripper. A discreet advert in the local paper should get things going.

DEAR BILL AND ZED,

Recently during work I have become somewhat "aroused" during meetings when talk is of "synergising strategies" and "blue sky thinking". When my supervisor suggested we should "park" my suggestion "offline" and "book some face time" later on, it was all I could do

BILL & ZED'S BAD ADVICE CONTINUED

to suppress an accident in my trousers. A strategically placed laptop spared my blushes! The final straw was when I found myself wistfully fingering a colleague's 100% polyester shirt and admiring their faux-leather safety shoes... What can be done?
Shipbuilder

ZED: Oh for God's sake, Shirley, just drop all the fey double entendres, get round there now and stick your fucking fist up his arse.

BILL: You are referring to a world I have no experience of and want nothing to do with. The fact that you work at a place that uses phrases like "synergising strategies" and "blue sky thinking" means that you are either stuck in a late nineties time warp or stuck way too far up your own arse.

If you have a soul worth saving, walk out on your job right now and don't bother with a letter of resignation. Just get out, sharpen your knives, and get on with your life. It is then that your true calling will become apparent. Once you are into double figures contact the pair of us to let us know how it's going.

DEAR BILL AND ZED,

Recently I have had to start commuting to work. I travel by train and my fellow passengers are middle-aged gentleman and ladies off for another day in the Big Smoke. The music on my iPod (Funkadelic and such like) makes me want to get off the train and go and smoke superskunk and get ripped like I used to, anything other than this daily ride with my rather depressing destiny. Can I get my mojo back, or is it gone forever?
Mojoless Man

ZED: Sorry friend but the fact that you actually have an iPod in the first place suggests to me that you never had a mojo to begin with.

BILL: You are a tosser. Anyone who uses a term like *mojo* and isn't Muddy Waters is a wanker and probably deserves to be reading magazines like *Mojo*. A magazine for men who have never amounted to anything but still want to believe in their teenage dreams of rock'n'roll freedom. You are shit. The music you listen to is shit. Your aspirations are shit. I just feel sorry for the "middle aged gentlemen and ladies" who have to put up with sitting on the train with you and your iPod. My advice to you is to petrol bomb the nearest newsagent to where you live that sells *Mojo*, and if anybody asks why, tell them Muddy Waters told you to do it.

DEAR BILL AND ZED,

I have recently fallen for a wonderful girl who exhibits all the traits an idler looks for in a partner—an inviting chest, a refined mind and a tolerant nature. However, this girl is currently involved with another man, a jazz performer, in a happy and stable relationship. How can I shake her from her complacent loved-up stupor and make her see that her so-called "happiness" is a total illusion and probably a bourgeois one at that?
Mopeyfrog

ZED: Well it seems to me you are obviously going to have to up the stalking techniques a gear or so. Why not interrupt one of jazz boy's performances one evening, heckling and insulting the sensitive fellow? This will obviously impress the big-titted pricktease no end and make her fall instantly in love with you.

BILL: Don't bother.

DEAR BILL AND ZED,

I fucked my boss even though he has a really tiny penis because he promised me a management position and a pay-rise but the wanker had me transferred to another department after he got it on with one of the boys from the mailroom and gave the position to him. Do you think I would have a case for sexual discrimination? Should I release the video I found in his house of him having it off with a garden hose?
Brendon 168

ZED: Two bumboy letters in one issue, what's going on here? You sound like one of Bill's special friends, Brendon dear fellow. I'll let my sensitive omnisexual colleague Billy Boy deal with you, not that I'm homophobic or anything and think that you lot should all be locked up in mental asylums, good Lord no, perish the thought, whatever made you think that?

BILL: I don't believe any of what you say. I don't know what your motives are for sending this letter into us or what advice you expect to get from us. You probably spend your days sending in bogus problems to all the advice columns in the hope someone will take notice of you. My advice to you is to shove the garden hose up your arse and turn the tap on full. Works for me every time.

DEAR BILL AND ZED,

I recently made a small change of job which has caused my overall salary to increase significantly without increasing my workload. But the extra income has caused my wife to think about knocking down the house and rebuilding it and she is now talking about boosting our monthly savings by two or three times. The whole thing is making me nervous. Should I conveniently lose my new job and go back to being broke?
JamesF

ZED: Good God, fuck all that shit Jimmy lad, and dump this mendacious slag immediately. Christ, she'll be wanting fucking kids next. Start your mid life crisis early.

Buy a Jag or a Harley Davidson, actually buy both and start knocking off women half your age immediately. Life is for living, bachelor boy. Go for it, stud!

BILL: Jobs? Salary? Workload? Savings? You're writing to the wrong column, mate. We know nothing of such things. We are Zen masters, not financial advisors. If in doubt, burn it down, is what I say. You should burn down that house of yours down and head for the nearest park bench with a can of Special Brew. 🐌

CONVERSATIONS

meiculo aouifee et si remeurne
de voftre deliurance monseigneur
de bourbon et monseigneur de
coucy car ilz ont moult fort en
tendu pour vous. Et aussi la
conteffe de saimt pol car la bon

ne dame sen ep
ment acquitte
Le seigne
pondy en telle
grant merci e
mais ie audoie

Comment les ioustes de saimt
Ingleuerch furent empuses, et
des faiz darmes par messire de
tnault de vyc messire bouchi
caulz le Jenne et le seigneur de
samt py.   Si.e

fut tresbel et b
Il auoit donne
damoiselles de
montxellier fi
et misee auant
lee lesquellee te
et la cause poi
la de nouueau
duny. Ser
ay commencie
vaillane cheua

E roy de france se
iournant en la bo
ne ville de mont
pellier en esbatemens et reuua?
ainsi comme il est cy desus

Ronald Hutton

TOM HODGKINSON **MEETS A MERRY PROFESSOR**

R onald Hutton teaches History at Bristol University. He specialises in late medieval history and the English Civil War. I first came across his work when I read that he had defended pagan protestor Arthur Pendragon in a court case. Later I read his book *The Decline And Fall of Merry England,* a brilliant account of how the old-fashioned festive culture of England was attacked by the new forces of Protestantism and Puritanism. Long-haired, mischievous and articluate, he is very popular with his students. Indeed, the catalyst for going to meet him was when I received two emails from former students, raving about what a brilliant lecturer he is, and urging me to go and meet him. One student told me that during his lecture on Christmas, he would gradually blow out candles until he himself disappeared with the final candle. His students would then find him crouching under the podium. A scholar and a showman, I was told.

IDLER: We're brought up to believe that the idea of Merry England is a myth, but the more I read the more it seems to be a concrete reality and fact. England was merry, the Protestants destroyed the festive culture and so I would say I'm anti-Protestamt and pro-Catholic.

HUTTON: I think you can be anti-Catholic as well. The Reformation and the Counter-reformation were two faces of the same movement by zealous Christians to tighten up Christianity and stop all this slackness and popular junketing. The Counter Reformation is much the same thing in Catholic guise. In other words there is more centralised authority, there's more emphasis upon the Bible and more emphasis on the chief figures in the Christian religion, and a clampdown upon local saints and on the tendency of ordinary people to take religion into their own hands.

IDLER: Is this something that's been going on since 1100?

HUTTON: It's more 1500 to 1600. It's part of a Reform movement which covers Western Christianity. It's the first big one that Christianity has had since the 12th century in which people who zealously want to get each other to heaven reckon that Christianity has got too slack, it's got too populist and popular. And people are enjoying themselves too much and not realising that they're probably going to go to hell as a result.

IDLER: This is a tendency in Western minds which grapples with the roustabout tendency.

HUTTON: It's also the Bible. There's not much that's relevant in the New Testament. It's a bit hard to imagine St Paul in a booze-up, but he does say, "take a little wine for thy stomach's sake."

IDLER: "Eat, drink and be merry" comes from Bible.

HUTTON: That's from Ecclesiastes, the great book that indicates you should enjoy yourself while you can, while being pious. But for every word in Ecclesiastes there are about ten ranted by the prophets. You need to read people like Amos and Habukuk [note from ed. I have now done this and he is right]. They are heavily against the kind of things that late medieval England enjoyed. Try to find the joke in the Old Testament.

IDLER: Is it very much late medieval England when things became really merry?

HUTTON: Yes, for two reasons. One is that it's the great age of community. It's a time when communities are under pressure. You have plagues sweeping the land repeatedly. You have traditional ways in which you hold land and work together in the village going to pieces because the population is plummeting. So there's a huge new stress on holding communities together in other ways. And one very good way to hold them together is to encourage them to have fun together. But the aspect is a complete reversal of the Church's traditional attitude to merriment. The traditional attitude, which is found in one invective after another from the beginning of Christianity through to the end of the 14th century, is to try and limit merry-making as much as possible because the consequences of getting boozed-up and sexy are almost unthinkable in moral terms. But towards the end of the 14th century the Church takes a new line and it seems to happen spontaneously because you don't get anybody organising a reform movement to bring it about. Its highlight is the 15th century. It is to co-opt merriment in order to pay for religion, in other words, to bring things like village feasts, dances and games into the orbit of the Church in order to make them into fund-raising events. So before this, the way in which you pay for your Parish church is the way in which it's been done for most of the time since the 16th century: you have a rate, you get people to rent a pew, or the church even owns its own lands which produces rents. But all this goes out in 1400 when the major means of raising the cash to pay for the candles, the incense, the vestments and the upkeep of the building is to hold a party, a sort of church fête but on a big scale. And all sorts of ways in which people had fun before this without any reference to the church, except when the church condemned them, now get brought into the orbit of fund-raising.

IDLER: Your own work is measured and academic but it's pretty obvious whose side you're on. You're pro-merry rather than pro-Puritan.

HUTTON: Yes. That's because I'm agnostic and so I can't personally see the point in the Reform's message. Because I don't believe in a heaven or a hell, the question of trying to save people from one and pump them into the other is irrelevant to me. So I'd rather see them enjoy themselves on earth. Now to a devout Christian, this is of course the devil's message. And I accept that, but since I don't buy the contrary message then I clearly am in the position you suggest.

IDLER: It wasn't a cynical move on the part of the Church?

HUTTON: Not cynical, it was sensible. If you follow their logic, and the logic comes out in their actions, then it's cheating the devil. The devil has set up things like boozing and dancing to lure people into sin, and now people are doing it in order to make Christianity more effective. The devil's been stripped of one of his greatest weapons, which is merriment.

IDLER: In Norman Cohn's *Pursuit of the Millennium* some of the medieval mystical sects go even further: to be really holy you have to free yourself of conscience, because conscience means you have the devil within you. So the truly pure can be free of conventional morality.

HUTTON: That's a tiny minority view. What I see as more representative is the line taken by someone like Richard Carew, St Anthony, who was a Cornishman who writes about Cornwall at the end of the 16th century, at a time when merriment has become deeply controversial again. Now the Reformation was the rejection of the religion which the merriment was supporting. What the merriment was doing was funding a very material religion, a religion heavy in props, a religion heavy in beautiful churches, incense, lots and lots of ceremony, beautiful clothes for the priest. These were supposed to make people think of heaven more easily and get to heaven more easily. And the Protestant message is that the whole theology at the foundation of this is wrong. You need to scrap all the very things that the fund-raising is supporting and fund preaching instead and so as they see it, the devil's scored a double whammy because he's actually corrupted Christianity itself and persuaded idiots to use his favourite weapons to support a wrong religion. He's almost got the jackpot. So Protestantism gets rid of medieval Christianity itself along with the fund-raising means that has supported it. So you're rejecting an awful lot together.

IDLER: Clearly there's something in the Puritan spirit which doesn't like people enjoying themselves. So what comes first? Is it the resentment at somebody else's having fun which then turns into a religion or is it the religion that happens to have as one of its components an attack on fun?

HUTTON: It varies from person to person. But if I put my money upon a majority view I'd go for the latter. Perhaps I'm being too generous. But for an agnostic I do know the Bible extremely well. I have read every word at least once with great care. And it's not a manual for party animals. There's an awful lot of condemnation of merry-making from jumping around the golden calf when your boss is up Mount Sinai onwards. So people who read the Bible regularly and use it as their basic text are going to be put off church ales really easily.

IDLER: Why has this particular period become one of your main areas of interest?

HUTTON: I think I got there originally because I was mesmerised by the English Civil War. Partly because it's the one time in the last 500 years when we've been really dysfunctional. And second because it's really glamorous: it's when we go to pieces and suddenly there's a violent resolution of traditional tensions all over the place which involves strongly marked characters, dramatic action, physical locations. It was riveting. And also it was in the air. In the 1960s when British society seemed to be going to pieces again, there was a huge interest. It's when these recreation societies got founded. It's the only time when the period hit the jackpot with a Hollywood blockbuster with Richard Harris in *Cromwell* and there were umpteen popular books on it. I was part of the generation that took to it. And it's spread out from that: I was interested in what made us rupture in the Reformation and again the Civil War in a way we haven't done since.

IDLER: What was the cause of the rupture? My line has tended to be that the simplistic, Cobbettesque one that the Reformation destroyed 900 years of brotherly love. It was a huge disaster created by the tyrant Henry VIII. But presumably there must have been something in the spirit of the nation that made us ready for this sort of change.

HUTTON: Well, it's a lot of nations, because we came quite late to it. And after all Henry VIII can be downgraded to a bit player because he produced a Catholic Church not a Protestant Church. So his son Edward and his daughter Elizabeth produced our real Reformations. They're part of a package which spans the continent. We get there after the Germans and the Swiss and the French and take up their ideas. We're in a corner of a big field. I think it's three things that happened physically and one thing that happened intellectually. There was a sense that the world was changing dramatically. It's difficult to believe the same things as your grandparents when the world isn't that of your grandparents. Now the Turks have bust into Europe, they're rolling back the borders of Christianity, so the idea of a medieval Christianity which is taking the world is reversed. Second, we invent printing which changes the face of communications, as big a revolution as the Internet now. Third, you have the discovery of new worlds beyond the sea into which we're expanding which give us a sense of manifest destiny to make up for the fact that Islam is munching away at the other side. And if I'd put in a wildcard I'd put in gunpowder which is blowing the face of warfare to pieces.

IDLER: Warfare is no longer a noble battle with elegance and rules.

HUTTON: Well it was always pretty horrible. It was always a butcher's yard with things like the longbow acting as the projectile system. But now you have to have huge armies, you have to have vast fortresses and you have to have standardised weapons going in to the hands of soldiers and they have to be made in factories. You have to have munitions dumps so again, even in the way you defend yourself it's a new world. So you

"THE REFORMATION AND THE RENAISSANCE ARE TWO FACES OF A HUGE RENEWAL OF EUROPEAN CULTURE"

put that lot together and people are getting really quite badly shaken up. And the way in which Christianity responds to this challenge of novelty is to come up with new ideas of its own. And that's because the late medieval Christian Church was extraordinarily dynamic. It was throwing off new ideas all the time. It was rapidly developing. And it was part of the movement that we call the Renaissance. It's Western civilisation going into overdrive.

IDLER: Was the Renaissance the flowering of medieval culture or the beginning of something new?

HUTTON: It was both. The Renaissance doesn't look like the Middle Ages. You can go back to the Middle Ages and find all sorts of antecedents for it. But there is a nationalism about, there is a new type of religion, that's Reformation and Counter-Reformation. There is a new style of communication, that's printing. There's a new concept of the globe, a new world, literally. The Reformation and the Renaissance are two faces of a huge renewal of European culture.

IDLER: And that's really what Shakespeare is all about, world on the brink.

HUTTON: For someone who was a dyed-in-the-wool conservative, Shakespeare's Dad was busted for Catholicism and Shakespeare probably spent time cosseted in a Catholic safe house in Lancashire when he was younger. It explains the sympathy with Catholics. It's very strange to find a Protestant playwright who looks with a kind heart on a friar like Friar Lawrence in *Romeo and Juliet*. Friars are seen as stormtroopers of the devil to a real Protestant. Shakespeare, like Ben Jonson, is somebody of really dodgy religion as far as a dyed-in-the-wool evangelical Prot–a hot Prot–is concerned.

IDLER: But wasn't he supposed to be producing propaganda for Elizabeth?

HUTTON: Yes, he also trims himself and he conforms and he is buried in his Parish church. Which he attended. He looks like a classic Church papist.

IDLER: Isn't there also this new idea, as in Dr Faustus, that you are in command of your own destiny, rather than a more fatalistic attitude that had gone before? Isn't there a new arrogance?

HUTTON: It's more desperation. When you live in a world, in a community of Catholicism which has got the truth long ago, and it's just a matter of working it out in individual terms, then you don't have that acute sense of danger and need to pull yourself together and get on. But if you're part of a what is a minority religion–Protestantism–which the existing religion wants to exterminate, and is actually starting to do so–in 1580 half of Europe is Protestant, in 1680 one fifth of Europe is Protestant–and Protestants are icrasingly forced into this area of Northern Europe so it's a nation like the Dutch and the English who take to the high seas desperately and try and make cash out of the rest of the world in order to survive.

IDLER: A bit like Jews who get pushed out and need to accumulate some money to provide safety.

HUTTON: Yes. I'd suggest a lot of the Protestant ethic is simply a survival strategy.

IDLER: Because you're being attacked. Now the Puritans, where did they come from? Do you turn into a Puritan? Or did

they come from outside and take over?

HUTTON: It's internal conversions. And it's almost a personality thing: you tend to find find that white-hot old style Catholics become white-hot new style Puritans. I define the Puritans as the Protestants in England who couldn't accept the compromised Church of England. They wanted to have one which was far more radically Protestant. We do have the least Protestant Protestant church in the world, because of Elizabeth's determination to secure a quick compromise. A church that's Protestant but contains a lot of Catholic features, we still have cathedrals after all, and bishops and robes for the clergy. And we have bits of the service that look very Catholic like making the sign of the cross and baptism.

IDLER: Christening services have something like an exorcism.

HUTTON: Yes and that's the kind of thing a Puritan would notice at once and really hate. So Puritans are simply the Protestants in England who are not only unhappy with the compromise but actually want to do something about it.

IDLER: Bertrand Russell said that the danger about them is that their will for change makes them dangerously executive. They will go and *do* things.

HUTTON: I think Russell was writing more about the Victorian Protestants than the early ones. But when you go back to the early modern period the Church of England is torn apart in a struggle between Puritans and those who loosely I'd call Anglo-Catholics.

IDLER: Meaning?

HUTTON: Those who happen to like the Catholic features in the Church of England and either want to keep them or even enlarge them, and the Civil War is largely the showdown, the shootout. Each wins in turn. The Puritans as we all know win in the Civil War, hence Cromwell, the chopping down of the maypoles and the abolition of church ales. But then the Anglo-Catholics come back in a big way with the Restoration and the monarchy. And it's the Puritans who are forced out of the church for ever. They become the Presbyterians, the Congregationalists, the Baptists, later the United Reformed Church and of course the Quakers, who are the people who wear black hats *par excellence*, to show that they are serious about going to heaven.

IDLER: The Quakers have a much more friendly image than the Puritans.

HUTTON: Well, not initially. Initially they are the stormtroopers of Puritanism, the most radical, the most reforming. It's just that they're turned upon so savgely by everyone else that they're forced to become pacifists and philanthropists and they do that extremely well. They've done it for 300 years and I think greatly enhanced our culture as a result. But they don't start out like that. They had a straight choice. Either they abandoned their radical views, or they persuaded those in power that they weren't a threat to them. And by becoming pacifists and suffering with extreme courage, without hitting back, they managed to survive.

IDLER: And who were the Puritans who went over on the Mayflower?

HUTTON: They were extreme Puritans who couldn't stand the established church. They wanted to found their ideal Church in the new land rather than put up with a compromise.

IDLER: And you see modern America as the result of that.

HUTTON: Modern America is the Puritan paradise. It's founded upon gathered churches, that is, churches that are not established by the State but paid for by the congregations. And communities form around them. There is a powerful ethic of the perfection and the improvement of the human race...

IDLER: Hard work...

HUTTON: Hard work but also Evangelism... interference, intervention.

IDLER: And how do you see Benjamin Franklin?

HUTTON: I see him as a classic example of the connection between socialism and Puritanism, meaning that the great reformers and progressive thinkers of modern times have often had an evangelical Protestant background, especially in Anglo-American culture. And if you're looking forward to the Gordon

Browns of this world, you'll find a lot of the socialist leaders are people with a background in Presbyterianism and Methodism.

IDLER: Why do they end up as socialists?

HUTTON: Because it's a part of reforming and perfecting society. And there's an awful lot in the Bible that you can actually put straight into socialism. These same prophets who are ranting against having fun are often ranting against the tyranny of kings and magistrates, and ranting against those who oppress the weak and the poor. And I remember Jesus saying a few things on a mount about the poor and the meek which are grist to the socialist mill. And rightly so. So the very people who are paying closest attention to their Bible about chasing out sin may well chase out capitalism as well.

IDLER: But The Sermon on the Mount is quite easy come, easy go. It's not about imposing your will on other people.

HUTTON: Yeah but read your Habukuk, the Biblical prophet. He's much more hellfire and brimstone against those who oppress.

IDLER: When the Protestant preachers came along and ranted against the profligacy of the established church, the people must have been feeling resentful already for the ideas to take root.

HUTTON: Some felt resentful, others were happy with it. There's always been this split in the Church of England between those who go into a church and ill-humouredly note the stained glass, and the altar cloth and latterly the polished cross and candlesticks, and think they're an affront. And those who wish the sermon would end so they can get on with communion, because that's the main thng for them.

IDLER: Going back to America, how would you say that Puritan project has turned out?

HUTTON: Huge success. Greatest power in the entire world. Again and again those who they face as mighty opponents seem to get overthrown without a huge amount of effort. In World War Two they find themselves useful allies at the right points and then the Warsaw Pact disintegrates which must be the hand of God.

> "A LOT OF THE SOCIALIST LEADERS ARE PEOPLE WITH A BACKGROUND IN PRESBYTERIANISM"

IDLER: When you go back to the early medieval period, I reecently read a theory that the 12th century is the most open.

HUTTON: I don't quite buy that. It's a great century of reform. It imposes celibacy on the clergy which to an agnostic does necessarily look like the best way of using human potential. It declares war on heresy, defines it and starts exterminating it systematically for the first time. For the first time the Church declares open war upon Islam and upon homosexuals. It's not my favourite kind of reform movement.

IDLER: Part of the medieval ethical approach comes from Aristotle which came through Arab translations. Is that right? In Southern Spain you get a mix of the two, mosques which are also used as Roman Catholic churches. That suggests that the medieval period was not only tolerant, it was actively interested in other people and other cultures.

HUTTON: I think it faces both ways and the 12th century is the best example of this. On the one hand medieval Christianity is very absorbant. It's forever taking new ideas and because of the explosion of Arabic learning there's an abnormally large number of them around the 12th century. On the other hand, whenever you get an explosion of new ideas the Church then polices the boundaries of what's acceptable. So on the one hand the 12th century is one of the most dynamic and enquiring and open of the medieval centuries, and on the other hand it's also one of the most oppressive.

IDLER: And nowadays that's what's confusing in protest movements: for example, I would see myself as pro-protest but then there's the unpleasant link between protest and reform and perfectionism and Puritanism.

HUTTON: Well it's the Sixties split, isn't it, which I remember all too well, between people on demos who had short hair and often beards, the men, and read their Marx and barked orders at you to get in line and told you what you had to believe. They didn't really seem to believe too much in democracy. And the long-haired rest of us who believed in individualism and choice were regarded by these snooty Marxists as self-indulgent traitors.

IDLER: When you see the May Day riots of today what do you see? A medieval spirit? Or a reforming spirit?

HUTTON: The Middle Ages are big on riots and so is the early Modern period. I think it's very medieval. It reminds me of the May Day riots—Evil May Day—in which they're rioting against foreign busi-

nessmen seting up in London and starting to make serious money. And later on in the 17th century every Shrove Tuesday you get apprentices on the street rioting just for the sake of it. But their targets were very clear: they rioted against brothels, they rioted against people who charged too much interest on their loans and going for the icons of capitalism is in many ways a direct descendant from that.

IDLER: Is it the spirit of Jesus turning over the tables of the money-lenders?

HUTTON: It is, but the great thing about the Bible is that it's so rich. The Jesus who flogs the money-changers out of the temples is the same one who tells you to turn the other cheek. On the one hand the Bible is an invitation to pacifism and quietism and on the other hand the Bible is an invitation to action. It all depends which fits your reading.

IDLER: You can read the Bible to defend idleness or to defend the creed of industry. But Jesus tends more towards the idle.

HUTTON: Basically the Bible is a handbook for a peasant and small craftsperson society. If you look at Jesus's parables that's what he understands. He's talking about peasant proprietors and people who are actually making things with their hands. Jesus's attitude to the Roman Empire is to render unto Caesar his due, because Caesar is basically not the point, he's too high and far off.

IDLER: It's about empowering the individuals here and now.

HUTTON: Well, I'd say the small man and woman.

IDLER: The medieval ploughman saw Jesus as his mate and companion.

HUTTON: That's absolutely correct. The Old Testament is very much that of hill farmers. The king who nicks someone's vineyard is someone who has colluded in the devil's work.

IDLER: That was an interest of Chesterton and Hillaire Belloc–they were into the idea of Distributism, where every family would have its own plot of land.

HUTTON: My answer to that was that it was all a bit late. We've been so totally restructured. What we can do in present day society is make the case that we can actually afford leisure as never before. So the movement to get us all to work harder than ever before and with more regimentation than ever before is totally unnecessary and artificial. We can do without it.

IDLER: It seems to be a Gordon Brown motivated sort of ideology.

HUTTON: Well, America had it first. It's the idea that you can actually perfect people. We can all do things better.

IDLER: That was New Labour's theme song, "Things Can Only Get Better". Things are always just about to get better and that actually serves the capitalist programme, because by buying things you are always just one step away. Whereas the Catholic thing seemed to be more, what we've got is the here and now, get on with living in the moment.

HUTTON: No, it's not Protestant and Catholic, it's modern and pre-modern. In a traditional society in which resources are fairly inelastic, there's much more emphasis on rubbing along with each other since you can't actually improve too much. The West invents the idea of Progress round about 1500 and nobody's quite sure why. It could just be all the things I've explained: a mass of new inventions, coupled with a deep insecurity that does it. China invents far more things than the West far earlier, but China goes to pieces every few hundred years and then reassembles itself with this massive stability. So it doesn't actually have this sense of being pushed to the edge that made it launch itself upon the sea. If China had ever been capable of having a Reformation, of having the kind of religion that produces one, and had been pressed by enormously powerful Mongols and Turks for about 500 years, then the Chinese would be all over the Americas by now. Well they are, but they'd actually own them.

IDLER: It's the energy that comes from being pushed.

HUTTON: That's the way I read it, it's the closest I can get to arguing from the facts. The truth is we don't have a history of Progress, meaning a modern reflective history of progress, we have lots of Victorian histories, regarding it as what's built in to

God's plan for the world.

IDLER: One of the things that motivates me in the *Idler* is a rage against the boredom of everyday employment.

HUTTON: It's a revolution that's happened in my lifetime. When I first went to work, as a civil servant in Whitehall, admittedly groomed for stardom since I had a Cambridge scholarship, back at the beginning of the 1970s, there was this sense of a kind of staple job that was laid out to leave the averagely productive person with a fair amount of spare time. It was up to you how you spent it. You could take longer lunch hours. Or if you were more idle than most, then the amount of work you were supposed to do would expand to fill the time, because you would work more slowly. If you were really ambitious you could ask for extra work, or you could catch up on your reading or file your nails. That's how people like Kenneth Grahame could be a clerk at the Bank of England and write *The Wind in the Willows* on the job. Slack was built in to what you were doing. That has all gone. We've had this revolution, everybody's been worked to the absolute limits and being checked up on the whole time. It's the age of assessment, surveillance… partly it's the technology, you can survey people… but there's this mentality that even if you can't you still need to issue questionnaires, fill forms, check up. Push, push, push. Clearly I'm an adrenalin-fuelled ambitious academic, so that sort of thing ought to fit in with me, and I'd rather see talent and ambition encouraged rather than squashed by drones, which was the problem with the régime thirty years ago, but it's still thoroughly unhealthy. I can see the results of stress all round me.

IDLER: What about your students? Have they changed?

HUTTON: Yes, they work enormously hard now. In many ways that's good for me, but the number of stress-related ailments they're producing, the amount of actual damage to their minds, is disturbing. Students didn't have personal problems thirty years ago, save the very occasional unlucky one. But now they are a recurrent feature of the tutor's realm.

IDLER: Going back to our theme of Protest and Idleness, what would your advice be to someone who wants to make their way in the world without becoming enslaved by the corporate megamachine?

HUTTON: It's very tough. Get together with like-minded people, read the *Idler*, and in your own life fight very hard for the right to work hard and by working hard create more space. In other words, fight as hard as you can to discourage those who employ you from observing that you've created some extra time by working extra hard and then filling it for you with yet more work.

IDLER: Shouldn't you work less hard?

HUTTON: It's very hard to do that in our current system. I would rather ring-fence work you can create for yourself. If you can make an agreement right at the beginning of how hard you work then nobody can push you unless you come up to the system already agreed.

IDLER: I was on the phone to someone the other day, and while we were talking he got an email from his boss saying: "please will you keep your phone conversations short and to the point as you may distract others in the open plan office."

HUTTON: Idiot. Replan your bloody office. ☻

Vive Le
Cinéma Flâneur

A TRIO OF FRENCH FILMMAKERS ARE ATTACKING
THE WORK ETHIC. CORINNE MAIER MEETS THEM.
TRANSLATION BY LAURENCE REMILA.

Pierre Carles, Christophe Coello and Stéphane Goxe are the French directors of the cult documentary *Attention Travail Danger* as well as *Volem Rien Foutre Al País* [a Provençal proverb meaning: "I can't be arsed doing anything in the country"], which is due for release in 2007. Pierre Carles and Stéphane Goxe took the time to be interviewed by Corinne Maier (author of the bestseller *Bonjour Paresse*).

CORINNE MAIER: Pierre Carles and Stéphane Goxe, you are the authors (along with Christophe Coello) of two side-splitting "anti-work" documentaries. Both ask this essential question: must you waste your life away trying to earn a living? The first, *Attention Travail Danger*

(2003), shows unemployed men and women happy with their lot and keen on remaining unemployed; the second, *Volem Rien Foutre Al País*, suggests alternatives to work that allow people to escape from the curse of "metro-boulot-dodo" (a French expression meaning "metro-job-sleep"). What exactly are you? Agitators? Lefties? Concerned citizens?

PIERRE CARLES: "Agitators", I'll take –if what you mean by "agitate" is to encourage reflection, to shake up all certitudes, clichés and received wisdom; in short, disturb the viewers, and get them to ask themselves questions they hadn't been asking–or, at least, not in those terms–and why not incite them –here, I'm speaking in my own name –to question the whole status quo. But I'd like to bring up an important point to start with: the first film allows "deserters from the workplace"–which I prefer to the expression "the happily unemployed"–the opportunity to express themselves. I'm not saying that because of some semantic coquetery. It seemed to us that first and foremost we were faced with individuals who'd deserted the battlefield where the "economic war" was taking place: men and women who no longer want to earn a living by wasting their lives away in degrading or poorly gratifying jobs, rather than people feeling really fulfilled thanks to their unemployment. It's more their direct or indirect experience of "wage-slave jobs" that's caused them to be disgusted with the world of work. As a result, they're less unhappy being unemployed than employed.

STÉPHANE GOXE: Personally, first and foremost, I feel driven by a very critical rapport to the world, which may be where my fairly pronounced taste for doubt and dissidence comes from. Taking that as a starting point, the documentaries I make are critical and are a non-dissimulated form of contestation of the established order.

MAIER: In both films, you go against the grain of the way work is usually thought of, denouncing the precarious nature of a lot of employment, crap jobs and the generalised exploitation of employees. Can you tell us more about that?

PC: It's difficult to summarise both films in a few lines. In the second one, *Volem Rien Foutre Al Païs*, we see certain aspects of the lives of those disuniting themselves, often collectively or semi-collectively, from capitalism. Besides those employees demonstrating their anger or the fact that they're fed up with the law of the liberal jungle, for example by burning down the premises of employers, there are also those who, using means that are less spectacular, less visible and more discreet, are also fighting the system by inventing or reinventing alternative modes of lifestyle. Those, as a general rule, question the dogma of productivism and aren't kneeling at the altar of economic growth–they're disputing the reign of the market. They're heretics, in the sense that they refuse to celebrate the cult of consumption, or to prostate themselves in front of the temples of consumption. Even if none of the groups or communities has found a generalised solution that can be applied to society as a whole, they invent–each at their level–other ways of living than those imposed by salaried employment, mostly in the countryside where it's easier to live autonomously and with very little money.

SG: From a cinematographic point of view, the theoretical denunciation of the submission to work has been stated elsewhere, for many years, very clearly. This critique was fairly present in the 1960s and 1970s, in film and in the critical debate, and it practically disappeared with the emergence of mass unemployment. The questioning that today's "social" cinema offers often limits itself to observing the dread caused by one's working conditions or the ruthless nature of the world of work. Basically, if this kind of cinema examines– and with what compassion!–the suffering in the workplace, it is less frequent that it asks questions about a life enslaved by the "necessity" of working, an existence that's suffocated by the yoke of "work, consume and die." It's this radical critique that we've tried to carry out with these two films.

MAIER: What are the French and

STILLS FROM THE WORK OF CARLES, COELLO AND GOXE

international anti-work movements (journals, associations, movements) that you're in touch with?

SG: Over the course of the five years of our investigations, we've met a bunch of people driven by this... critical "work", in France, Spain and Germany... We've had a lot of contact with the Barcelona group, Dinero Gratis.

PC: If we had to name just one source of inspiration, it would probably be "L'An 01", the comic and film by Gébé, the great utopian cartoonist whom we were lucky enough to meet shortly before his death.

MAIER: It's possible to treat *Volem Rien Foutre Al Païs* as if it were a veritable Decalogue: you will work as little as possible; you will consume as little as possible, you will find ingenious and ecological ways of being independent of the multinationals; you will rob major companies because they rob you; you will requisition unoccupied housing; you will support your fellow non-worker. Is that a political programme?

PC: A "programme", surely not. But it all depends on what you mean by "political". If you have a conception of the "political" as being a noble activity, not all about authority, where nothing is thought to be impossible or inconceivable right from the start, and if we set the condition that these choices are freely consented to, without there being anyone in the collective feeling ripped off, then why not? We can't really deny that *Attention Danger Travail* and *Volem...* are films that affirm a political viewpoint. At the same time, each and every film is political. Particularly those that don't state the fact that they are and claim to be apolitical (like TV series or the news). We can but hope that *Volem...*, while being open about its political position and not trying to hide its politically-engaged view of the social world, isn't part of some new catechism. The temptation is there: "degrowth" is a fashionable movement, and its concept of "voluntary simplicity" is intellectually tempting, especially for those who no longer know where to turn, but the film's producer Annie Gonzalez and its editor Roger Ikhlef made sure that the film didn't provide a moralising or pious discourse about these practices. The film simply shows that lifestyles other than those we constantly see on TV, in advertising or in the major media outlets, are possible. It also disassociates itself from a new genre of documentary we're seeing: the compassionate film that says: "Look how these workers and employees made redundant by the head of some

FROM VOLEM RIEN FOUTRE AL PAIS

multinational suffer. Let's suffer together." While acknowledging that social reality, we've tried to approach it more as dreamers and perhaps be more subversive by concentrating on the different utopias, and not preachifying.

SG: Yes, it's a political programme, and we intend to sell it to the highest bidder... Well, the film is openly political, but it's not–in my opinion–the role of a film to be programmatic. Besides, this film raises more questions than it provides answers. For some people, what you call "Decalogue" is nothing more nor less than a programme... for living, while for others it's a struggle at the periphery of the dominant ways of thinking... But in both cases, it's a question of reappropriating one's means of existence, to regain–at least to some extent–the possibility of living one's life as one chooses. Such aims don't seem soluble in any kind of electoral or "good citizen" preoccupations.

MAIER: There are aspects of *Volem...* that evoke certain communitarian utopias from the 1970s; is your film a "revolution" (in the sense of returning to that same place) or are you taking that same theme from back then so as to create something else?

PC: It's more of a reformulation of the question posed by the desertion of the workplace. If one isn't born wealthy, if one isn't a trust-fund baby and wants to escape from salaried work or work as something one's forced to put up with, it's best to join forces; to help each other and work collectively. It may seem obvious to say it, but it's worth not overlooking the fact that there's "strength in unity". That's sometimes achieved through living in a community, but not exclusively. One can find collective efforts and solidarity elsewhere than in the few communities in existence today–communities that don't really resemble those from the 1970s. For example, we never came across examples of "free love", of fusional practices or of multi-partner sex, which were all tried and tested back in the 1970s. It's become very well-behaved, as far as that kind of thing is concerned.

SG: *Volem...* doesn't invent anything so to speak, but the context has changed drastically. The film reformulates, in contemporary terms, a radical critique of the society of work and merchandise, such as was carried out by previous generations. *Volem...* is less about categorical affirmation and its tone is probably darker (which suits the era we're living in) than the flowery utopias bandied about in the

"THE DOCUMENTARY SHOULD QUESTION REALITY AND QUESTION THE CONDITIONS OF EXISTENCE"

1970s. It's less about ideology than it was back then, that's for sure. I don't think the people we filmed are nostalgic for that period, but they are keen on exploring once more paths that have already been taken, such as the collective adventure, which today is widely revisited but which it would be best to distinguish from the communal experience pursued feverishly back then. Also, the issue of individual and collective autonomy, which thirty or forty years ago could be seen as merely an option of social organisation, now appears to some as the only way out. "We no longer have the choice," exclaims one of the people filmed. "It's merchandise...or life!"

MAIER: How have your films been financed and distributed?

SG: Up to now, these films have existed without any institutional aids or money from TV channels, and despite this they've been shown in cinemas, thus generating their own resources (yup, we're in the market economy as well...). With *Volem*, we obtained aid from the CNC (France's Centre National de la Cinématographie which grants money to film productions, using their expected future box office earnings to calculate the amount) for the first time. We also benefited from some public funding. There won't be a shortage of zealots to judge whether or not this money has led us to moderate our discourse, to make the film more socially acceptable...

PC: I'd like to add that France's network of independent movie-houses, unique in the world because of its density, allows documentaries to enjoy a near-nationwide release: these can be new documentaries, or those not allowed broadcast access on the small screen—which was the case for the four I directed since 1998, and which have been fairly successful at the cinema. They've each attracted an average of 90,000 spectators—a figure that's more than respectable for a documentary film.

MAIER: What do you consider the role of a documentary film?

SG: To question reality. That's not its only function, but we personally approach it as a means of questioning reality such as it's presented to us, or such as we see it unassisted. At the same time, it serves to question our conditions of existence. It should also perhaps serve to suggest, formally, new ways of representing the world. And the documentary is also a critical act fundamentally relevant to expressing anger, despair, laughter...

MAIER: What can be done to change society? Can a possible recourse to violence be legitimate?

SG: The question can be asked, of course, but in my opinion it's not here and now that I can or would want to answer it.

PC: And I don't have the legitimacy to answer these questions. But obviously, the question gets asked. Within certain groups filmed for *Volem...*, people are asking these questions. This question is also addressed in one of my most recent films *Ni Vieux, Ni Traîtres* (co-directed with Georges Minangoy), particularly by people close to the Action Directe group who'd hoped to change the world through armed revolt. Without success.

CM: Please tell us about your other films: Pierre Carles, amongst your many activities, you've directed two films that are very critical of the media, *Pas Vu Pas Pris* and *Enfin Pris?*. Can you tell us about them? And Stéphane Goxe, can you tell us a little bit about yourself?

PC: In *Pas Vu Pas Pris* (1998) and *Enfin Pris?* (2002), we examine the problem of the subtle or very obvious censorship that's at work in the French media. These films were boycotted by French television, which is one of the reasons why they set records in terms of illegal downloads on the internet. But it's not forbidden to buy the DVDs of them and thus support our independent productions! It's the money made thanks to the release of *Pas Vu Pas Pris* that allowed the production of the only documentary portrait of the sociologist Pierre Bourdieu while he was still alive. As for *Attention Danger Travail*, it was partly made thanks to a subscription launched before to release a shorter video version of the film, thus offering a preview of it.

SG: I've made films that are to do with experiences of popular resistance, particularly in South America (*Mari Chi Weu*, all about the struggle of the Mapuche Indians in Chile; *Tu n'es Pas Mort Avec Toi*, all about how the children of the dictatorship fight against political impunity in Argentina). But they are also films that try to shake the vision of the situation in those countries, generally imposed by the media, that we have in Europe; films that, while refusing all exoticism, try to show the links between the mechanisms of repression and domination that are at work on both sides of the ocean (it's the case of "Chile, dans l'ombre du jaguar").

MEIER: What are your projects?

PC: I've just finished a documentary about "Professor Choron", the founder of the magazines *Hara Kiri* and *Charlie Hebdo*, which I co-directed with the cartoonist Martin. Choron and his gang of cartoonists played a similar role in France to Monty Python in the UK. A year and a half after his death, we want to pay him tribute; part of the reason is that certain comedians, who owe him almost everything, deny the importance of his work. With my producer Annie Gonzalez, we have two other film projects: one all about "the end of the world"; another about the way the major private Venezuelan media tried to help oust the elected president, Hugo Chavez, while at the same time trying to see if such an attempt at a media "coup d'état" could take place in Europe. Finally, I have an "old" project, with my wife, which we'll get underway one day: a film about the French singer Nino Ferrer.

SG: In the immediate future, I'm going to work on something shorter, a sort of "cine-tract". As for later, we'll see, but I have to say I'm fascinated by the efforts —sometimes pathetic and desperate—of the "system" to get us to adhere to some of its increasingly contested and forsaken values. What else are we expected to swallow, just how great will the distance between reality and its representations become? The idea would be to examine the grotesque aspect of this barbarism; it could result in a film both absurd and frightening. ☻

In Conversation With:

Green Gartside

ANTHONY REYNOLDS MEETS GREEN FROM SCRITTI POLITTI, FIFTY YEARS WITHOUT A PROPER JOB

IDLER: How are you?

GARTSIDE: Oh, I'm in some kind of state where a battle between a hangover and a virus is taking place

IDLER: Jeez... what a combo... A virus and a hangover... one of the worst afflictions that I suffer from is hayfever and hangover combined...

GARTSIDE: Oh yeah? I get hayfever too...although not as bad as I used to. Don't you take... stuff for it?

IDLER: Yeah I do but... people respond to treatment differently... it doesn't always work...

GARTSIDE: I was like that as kid. In fact, I... it was annoying...I used to get it so badly that... do you remember that they once decided that they had a cure for hayfever?

IDLER: Oh yes, I had an experience of this.

GARTSIDE: They used to give injections and I had to go to the Gwent Hospital in Newport every Saturday morning –imagine this when you're a kid–you think you're gonna get to the weekend and it'll be yours but you had to go up to the hospital. This went on for months, every Saturday morning, I'd go up for an injection. Ach! And it never worked. It was supposed to get you ready for the next summer and you weren't supposed to get hayfever for the next summer. And I did that two winters running. What a waste of time.

IDLER: I had exactly the same experience. I had to go to my GP and it was as you say, horrible. What little kid wants a needle in his arm? There's a joke there somewhere... anyway... the doctors... they just stopped suddenly. Some kid fell over and sprouted fur all of a sudden and it was like "Oh we're gonna stop this now, please don't tell anyone..."

GARTSIDE: [Laughs]

IDLER: But the bugger with hayfever is that every year I forget that I suffer from it. So I kind of wade into the beautiful blooming summer and then I notice I'm sneezing and my eyes are aflame... and it's like, "Oh yeah, I don't belong in this season..." all over again.

GARTSIDE: I used to take ant-hista-mines and they would really knock you out.

IDLER: I always ask specifically for the drowsy anti-histamines, 'cos I like being doped up.

GARTSIDE: Yeah... doped up...That reminds me. I was talking to Mark Rad-cliffe the other day, and he'd come from a John Cooper Clarke and one of the ex members of the Fall... they are doing gigs as a duo at the moment. And they're both ex junkies and on the rider for the gig they have a bottle of Scotch each and two bottles of Benylin cough syrup each. And Radcliffe said he went into the dressing room and the ex Fall guy was appalled... and he was going... "Non fooking drow-sy! Non-fucking drowsy! How could they give two fookin' Ex Junkies non drowsy Beneylin!" Which I thought was good.

IDLER: Ah, yes....The eternal dilem-ma...the difference between day and night nurse...

GARTSIDE: Yes, well, you know...

IDLER: You know about Ray Charles? When he was off heroin and he came up with this... he was like a chemist...he came up with this concoction... which was... brandy, mixed with nicotine and really sugary coffees. And it enabled him to work because he said it had a similar effect on him as junk.

GARTSIDE: Hmm.

IDLER: I believe you live in East Lon-don now, but didn't you live in the coun-tryside for a while?

GARTSIDE: Yeah, well, I moved to Usk. A cottage there. But yeah I know what it's like to live rurally. All I ever did was go up the pub and buy music. I didn't bother wasting money on food or anything.

IDLER: Your latest album, *White Bread Black Beer*... that's my introduction to your work.

GARTSIDE: Oh really, that's interesting.

IDLER: And I don't want to embarrass you, but it blew my balls off.

GARTSIDE: Gosh. [Silence] I guess that's good?

IDLER: I guess that must be interest-ing for you because... when I got into it, I thought, "Well I remember this guy vaguely..."–'cos you can't be fans of everyone, as you know... I had some awareness of Scritti Politti... but then... I was worried, 'cos the older I get I worry that I won't be as open to having my balls blown off by new music... I'm kind of secretly worried that I'll lose my pas-sion for new music. Do you know what I mean?

GARTSIDE: I do. And I haven't lost my passion for music. And it'd be fucking awful the day that it does go. You know, when you no longer get excited about something or want to check something new out. But I guess there's a lot of peo-ple my age that still listen to music but kind of... I don't know... they just don't go looking for anything new. You know what I mean?

IDLER: I'm a big Miles Davis freak and so when I went back and found *Cupid and Psyche* in a charity shop in the village and so I got to hear "Perfect Way" with vocals. It was so weird.

GARTSIDE: Oh yeah, it would be weird. I haven't listened to it since I made it so... see, we're off to America in a couple of weeks and I've a horrible feeling that people in America will shout out for old songs. Which is… er… I never know how to feel about that: whether you should oblige the people by playing a few or a lot. But anyway, we decided as a band that we'd have a listen to "Perfect Way" tomorrow…

IDLER: That was a hit in America, right?

GARTSIDE: That was the one big hit– Pop hit anyway–in America, so…

IDLER: You even did it on the Dick Clarke show, right?

GARTSIDE: Yeah. American bandstand, that's right. A lot of madness. That's when it started to go pear-shaped for me. I can remember that very day that it was: "Hang on this is not really the right line of work for me," that's what I thought. From that point in time 'till I was back in Usk a few years later… it just felt wrong. I thought I'd enjoy being a pop star and I was messing around with "pop music" but I wasn't really, I was just a bit of product. It wasn't fun. I stopped at that point finding it amusing. It was the insincerity that really fucking pissed me off. They don't really care. It was just ruthless and heartless and it'll do your fucking head in, I reckon. It did mine in anyway.

IDLER: It must be difficult to temper your reaction. 'Cos I guess you don't want to to be rude to these people…

GARTSIDE: Oh, I was always concerned with being "nice", I just wanted to please these people. When you're brought up to be polite and deferential and always be… we had to do lots of American television and it was lots of chat show type things.

> "I THOUGHT I'D ENJOY BEING A POP STAR. BUT I DIDN'T. I WAS JUST A BIT OF PRODUCT, REALLY"

We weren't playing live so they said, "well then you can do all this telly and radio instead". And after a few months of it you really end up hating yourself deeply, I think. You hate everybody around you and you hate yourself for talking so much bullshit. You try not to but you end up doing it.

IDLER: Did you ever consider getting fucked up and doing it?

GARTSIDE: Oh yeah, I tried that. There was a fair bit of substance and alcohol abuse to get you through some of that time and that certainly didn't help in the long run. You can become badly unstuck. I remember doing some radio sessions –even here in the UK and being too fucked up to actually do them. But anyway that's all, happily, consigned to the past.

IDLER: that leads me to your new album. I'm someone with no prior knowledge of you and your work but I was listening to it a lot before I looked at the lyrics and one of my first impressions was: "this sounds like a record made by someone who is a bit of a booze hound". There's a fantastic line in one of the songs that says–well, I thought it said, "racking in the kitchen". And I was kind of disappointed when I looked at the lyrics and it said "Rockin".

GARTSIDE: Oh! Sorry about that.

IDLER: That asides, is it a true perception or am I completely off the page?

GARTSIDE: No, no, there are tons of references to… there's a lot of… you don't realise because you write them a song at a time and then you come back and... I remember I had to write them out for Rough Trade and thinking "fuck me, there's a lot of recurring themes." A lot of alcohol, there's a lot of references to "fathers"... which I hadn't realised I'd done...there's a lot of stuff going on in one's subconscious. So it's interesting to look at the lyrics and think: "Blimey! You are just an old lush who has unresolved issues"! [Laughs]

IDLER: Sure... some of the lyrics seemed so graphic to me. Like almost as if... it had reached a point where it was "Stop drinking or else"—in terms of your health.

GARTSIDE: Uh...yeah...

IDLER: You don't have to talk about any of this stuff...

GARTSIDE: No, no, it's fine. What would be the best thing to say about that. Hmm. It's certainly a question that's crossed my mind. Put it that way. And you will gather that since I'm talking to you with a hangover and a virus, I am still enjoying my beer to the full! I guess one thing I have down is like, when we play live or anything... and we haven't done much touring but we've done some and Japan and stuff... and I just do all of those tours completely sober. There's no way I can be... it's the only way I can do it, do you know what I mean?

IDLER: Are you like James Brown? Are the other guys not allowed to drink? Do you fine them if they turn up fucked?

GARTSIDE: Oh no, everyone can... and they do! Believe me. My band likes to party, so... that's kind of weird. There is that thing of after the gig I'll go and have something to eat with them, then they'll go clubbing, and I'll go back to the hotel.

It's just the wise thing to do.

IDLER: Sure. Some people would know that but wouldn't act on it.

GARTSIDE: Fortunately I've got enough self-discipline to hold that together so I'm all right. Touring is hard work but good fun.

IDLER: Going back to lyrics, I read an interview where you said that introspection and looking back on things didn't serve you well. I would have thought that these traits would be prerequisites for any songwriter.

GARTSIDE: Ah. I guess what I mean is that I don't do it in the course of ordinary life. I never ever think about the past and I got a stinking memory anyway. I don't like to think about the past. I never have, I remember as a kid memories would come into your head and they would be almost physically painful. So, you learned to be actively forgetful and not think about the past. It's become a habit... there's either stuff in your past that was painful and you didn't want to remember it or there were things in your past that were good so you'd be sad that they had gone. So I go through life not really considering the past which means I don't have a very good sense of time which means you can spend years near Usk not doing anything and it doesn't matter. But when it comes to songwriting I suppose you just sit down and it all comes out without you having to go and look for it. And I like it with lyrics where you jump from very specific things, almost physical things, specific memories of peoples and places and then you suddenly find that the next line you've written has

"I DO HAVE AN INCREDIBLE ABILITY TO DO NOTHING"

more to do with something you got from a book that you read or some other lyric that you heard and then that leads your mind onto some other memory of a place and a feeling and the whole thing just shifts back and forth... between the specific and the abstract.

IDLER: Yeah. And it really did it for me. Lets talk about sloth. I think that smoking a spliff, drinking Budvar and watching TV all day is a talent. Have you got that talent?

GARTSIDE: I do have an incredible ability to do nothing. I've gone fifty years without ever having a proper job and spent a lot of that time doing absolutely nothing except maybe reading books and going to the pub. And I can happily sustain that for my remaining years... the only thing is the occasional bout of boredom and that's best alleviated either by making some music or getting off your face. And that's possibly... if anyone were to say "What's your singular achievement?", I suppose it was to manage to get through life without doing a proper job. I guess as long as at some point you feel that you want to get off your arse and do something it seems to me that if work is only some months out of a year and you can get away with it, that's all right. Its perfectly acceptable isn't it?

IDLER: I guess it relates to money doesn't it?

GARTSIDE: Yes, that's true. But the key thing is not to be acquisitive about money. If you're content to have just enough to pay the rent and keep the wolf from the door and you don't think about the future —which is something else I don't do. I've made no provisions for my future whatsoever. If you just sort of... just don't think about it, it seems quite easy to live cheaply and simply.

IDLER: When you kind of "retired" then, and lived in Usk, what did you live off? Was it royalties from your 1980s work?

GARTSIDE: Yeah. There would always be, much to my amazement just enough. But also, back when I left Rough Trade and signed to the majors, I made sure that I did split world deals and split world publishing deals and I had very good lawyers and managers who really got me an awful lot of good deals. And it was as a consequence of being given silly amounts of money that was sloshing around in the 1980s. Between that and royalties... it kept me going for a very long time. I guess, slowly *Cupid and Psyche* must have sold enough copies around the world to keep me afloat. And it's still true today, to my amazement. You know, you get a cheque from a publisher every now and then and you think: "Christ—that's all right then. That's another six months looked after! And as long as you don't look beyond that, it's all right. But if you look beyond that and think: "How the fuck am I going to live in ten years' time?" you may freak out... but I don't even think about it.

IDLER: OK. I'm just gonna make a jump here... you have a problem with Eddie Mare? [BBC Radio 4 news presenter]

GARTSIDE: Yeah I do! He drives me mad! He annoys the fuck out of me. He used to do a news thing on Radio 4 on a weekend morning... *Broadcasting House* it was called and he was just... Oh man, don't get me started on Eddie Mare. He's too fucking flippant. He's too smug. He should be on commercial radio doing a phone in or whatever... he can't make up his mind if he wants to be John Humphries or Jimmy Saville... and he's equal to neither of them! [Laughs] I don't know what I'm talking about now. 🞄

FEATURES

Eat the Rich

WHEN THE YALI PEOPLE OF PAPUA FOUND
THEMSELVES UNDER ATTACK, THEY REVERTED TO
AN OLD-FASHIONED WAY OF DEALING WITH THEIR
OPPRESSORS: THEY ATE THEM. BY JAY GRIFFITHS
ILLUSTRATIONS BY GEORGIA HARRISON

t was a Sunday in Jayapura, the capital of West Papua. I was at a loose end and decided to go and tease missionaries. I went to an American fundamentalist service, and met Linda, who talked to me about her church's early travails here. Her eyes blue and round as a child's, she said: "Our first two were martyred by the Yali people several years ago." What happened? I asked. The carriers didn't want to go on, she told me, but the missionaries had insisted, and so the carriers killed them. "They were *eaten*," she said in an appalled whisper.

"Oh," I said, trying to be diplomatic. "Did that put you off a bit?" Silly question. Missionaries had come flocking here after that, she said. "It spurred people on to come here because of the darkness that these people were obviously living in." It was, she said, "a spiritual darkness that is a wilderness." She nodded and blinked. "Just our presence there sheds light to the people," she said, self-effacingly.

"Did you tell them," I asked sweetly, absolutely determined to quote Flanders and Swann, "did you tell them that *Eating People is Wrong*?"

She missed the reference, but apparently told Papuans that many things were wrong with them. Wearing penis gourds. Keeping their religious objects. Thinking mountains were sacred.

I had gone to West Papua to research a book on wilderness and ideas of the wild. I was interested in land rights and freedom, and the wild, often unmapped mountains of West Papua called me. That and an almost unreported genocide.

Wilderness was also what the fundamentalist missionaries sought—sought not to preserve it but to destroy it. In West Papua, they pray for "untouched" "interior" places to be "opened up" with airstrips and mission stations. While the Catholic church seems sometimes to work for the benefit of Papuans, the activities of the evangelical fundamentalist sects appalled me; and my expectations were low to begin with. One missionary said that the Papuans were "controlled by evil spirits". Commented another: "They are about as natural as you can get: they have no concept of God," which seemed to me a pretty fair illustration of the opposition between their god and nature. "After conversion", ruminated a pastor from Ohio, "they would no longer be–" he hesitated–"I hate to use the word savages, but, you know, savages..."

Europeans have long been fixated by savages, cannibals and head-hunters, buzzing with a self-delighting frisson of horror. I've spent a delightful weekend with cannibals and the descendant of head-shrinkers is a good friend of mine. One of my questions, was simple: who are the savages?

One answer came quickly: a friend, Sure-yani Poroso, told me of the ritual head-shrinking practised by his tribe, the Leco people in Bolivia. "We recorded our history in trophies of shrunk heads to teach children to defend our culture. The Catholic church prohibited head-shrinking, and called us savages for doing this but we shrunk the heads of those who had tried to destroy us–we had good reasons for killing them. The real savages are those who kill without reason, the rubber barons in the past, the capitalism of today." (And the recruiting sergeants for today's genocidal corporations are called what? Head-hunters.)

Indonesia was land-hungry and wanted West Papua for its acres and for its wealth of natural resources, and in 1962 it invaded and began the mass murder ignored by most of the world. Papuans wanted their freedom. Too bad. Instead their villages were bombed and napalmed. Women were raped and men tortured. The colonial power, the Netherlands, had tried to give West Papua independence but America had had other ideas. For geo-political reasons, the U.S. wanted Indonesia to take the country– "a few thousand miles of cannibal land" was how Robert Komer, J.F. Kennedy's CIA adviser was to describe it.

Amnesty International suggests that the death toll could be 100,000 people, out of a population of perhaps two million. This genocide suits America and Britain very well, as Indonesia gives their corporations licence to steal Papuan resources, but there's another thing: the genocide is irresistibly lucrative for the arms trade. In 2002, UK arms sales to Indonesia reached £41 million. That's about a quid from every adult. Every bloody one of us.

• • •

All over the world, mountains have long been considered sacred–it seems to be a human constant. In West Papua, mountains are the place of the ancestors and a place of "dream shrines" where people can go to find a dream to guide them.

I met a rainmaker in his hut, surrounded by feather crowns, bows and arrows and tins of pilchards. Old, talkative, toothless and blind, he told me that there are no gods close to the village, but away up in the hills, where the mountain is wild, there are gods. I asked him about the missionaries and mining. "I'm really angry about that," he said. "When villages become Christian, they want mines, and it's not good to mine the mountain. Here, we don't want mines; the power of the mountain spirit keeps the soil, plants and animals healthy." I heard this everywhere: in villages which were still animist, no mining was allowed, but in Christianised villages people wanted to exploit and sell the land's resources.

When the missionaries came to West Papua, the currency was the cowrie shell. Missionaries brought an enormous number of shells, causing a crash in the value of the cowrie. And the huge numbers of steel axes which they brought knocked the bottom right out of the stone axe market. The missionaries came from the sky in helicopters full of goods which Papuans had never seen. To them, the astonishing arrival of goods from the air triggered a wave of cargo cults including one group who fervently believed that a bicycle pump thrust in the ground would result in the emergence of goods. Asking one man why his village became Christian, I was told simply: "Because the missionaries brought metal axes and knives and mirrors." People identified this new god with goods and became Christians to get the goods.

But the local people have been short-changed in the bargain. They remain dirt poor, while the resources of their lands enrich the invaders.

In West Papua, the missionaries openly support the corporations. One told me plumply how they helped an oil company to build a runway, that the oil companies want missionaries in their area "to keep the situation stable" and that the missionaries happily oblige. In Ecuador, missionaries from the Summer Institute of Linguistics (S.I.L.), a very right-wing American missionary outfit responsible for cultural genocide, lured Huaorani people into a reservation, helping Texaco blaze a mining trail through their lands and opening the area to colonization.

Mission airstrips are used by the Indonesian government, with the full blessing of the missionaries. S.I.L. missionaries preach submission to the State. Any State. Even a genocidal one.

I was taken to meet a group of freedom fighters from the OPM (Organisasi Papua Merdeka, the Papuan Freedom Movement). They had faith, they said, that if people knew of the genocide here, the outside world would help. They had faith in the international media, in the United Nations, in politicians. The one group of people in whom they have no faith whatsoever is the Christian fundamentalist missionaries. The missionaries do not care about Papuan freedom and independence, said the commander, because the missionaries support the murderous Indonesian government which, in turn, supports the missionaries. I was to meet dozens of such missionaries in West Papua, and only one thought that the Papuans should be free in their own land.

Some Papuans have declared missionaries one of the four greatest threats to ecological and cultural survival. The Christian Missionary Alliance, Papuans tell me, prays for the success of Freeport, the mine which has the worst record for human rights abuses of any in the world.

For the local Amungme people, who live near the Freeport mine, their mountain is a spiritual realm. On their mountain, old and sacred groves may never be destroyed and when their ancestors died, they told me, the souls travelled to the mountains. Death translates them into land, so the ancestors merge, through metaphor and in spirit, with mountain. The mountain is the embodiment of "the mother" in a beautiful example of sacred geography. The mountain top is her head, and is holy; her feet reach the sea, fifty miles away.

Freeport is mining the mother. The jutting JCBs come, sinking a mine shaft, drilling into her head, against her will, a head-fuck. And the rivers which once ran with the mother's milk now are dank with deadly toxicity. This mountain, this woman is the quintessential "interior" that the missionaries want "opened up." Open her legs for the mining company, entering the prohibited area where they will shove their drillbits and tailings. The taboo lands of her thighs, which traditionally people are not allowed even to see, have been seized by Freeport as the place to dump their toxic sludge. The Amungme people have experienced psychological problems they did not know before: "they, especially the tribal leaders, cry just like children," I was told.

"I am witness by my eyes," said a Papuan man who lived near the Freeport mine. And his story left me devastated. When he was in elementary school, he saw a hundred or more people tortured, the Indonesian soldiers forcing iron rods in their ears. He saw needles stuck in people's eyes and people killed, axed in the head. He saw the soldiers putting iron rods in fires till they were red-hot, and shoving them up people's anuses. People were killed that way, he said, as you would kill rabbits. Technically, these abuses are carried out not by Freeport but by the Indonesian military acting to "protect" the mine. So murder is contracted-out. Rape is outsourced. It's good business practice.

These kinds of tortures are attested to by other sources and human rights workers around the Freeport mine. Thousands of local people have been made homeless by Freeport. Hundreds, possibly thousands, have been murdered. Savages, head-hunters, cannibals.

A couple of weeks after meeting Linda, the missionary, I was in the Highlands with Yali ex-cannibals, who had, after that dodgy start, since converted to Christianity. I met the local villager who was now the priest.

"What happened with the missionaries?" I asked. The story flooded out. Missionaries had invaded their village. The Yali people were terrified and ran away into the forests. The missionaries chased them, as if hunting them, and the Yali people fled again, frightened, further into the forests. A third time the missionaries came after them, and this time the Yali people couldn't take it anymore, got their bows and arrows and shot them. And then ate them. It seemed quite reasonable to me.

The priest had been eight or nine at the time and everyone was a cannibal then. (Since the village turned Christian, they no longer eat anyone except Jesus, and him only on Sundays.) "What did it taste like?" I asked. "It tastes a bit like beef," the priest is quite happy to tell me. "And," he went on, "when we killed and cut up the missionaries to eat, one missionary was too fat and didn't taste good so we used him as fire-lighters." For the record, I did try not to laugh.

• • •

"Go and talk to Tarzan," I was told by several people in the Peruvian Amazon. "Ask him about the missionaries." Tarzan, a Harakmbut man in his nineties, remembered the time when the missionaries first came to his lands.

"The missionaries came in a plane which," said Tarzan, "we thought was a huge and frightening eagle, of a type we'd never seen before. We fled to the hills. Every day, the missionaries came searching for us. When the plane saw us, it flew very low, which was all the more frightening. The plane dropped machetes and sweets and clothes and mirrors. It frightened us, and we didn't use them. We did try to sow the sweets like seeds but of course they never grew."

Tarzan was old, so steeped in years that even the old men called him *tío*–uncle–as they nodded in keen agreement with Tarzan's memories. Tarzan went on: "We took our arrows and tried to shoot it–we did think we'd hit the plane's backside." They remembered it all perfectly, and the old men leaned back, as if re-enacting it all, shooting arrows of the past, at a plane long flown, in a sky unchanged.

Before the contact, "everything was good for us, the plants and animals and fish. We lived *fuerte*, strong; we wore no clothes, only feathers. We were painted and singing." Was life better then? "There were no illnesses, worries or problems. Of course life was better then, *antiguamente*. We were rich in what we were."

The missionaries set up a mission station and a school. "We were scared and threatened by them," said Tarzan. "No one wanted to go to school, and anyway after the missionaries came, our children died. We learnt things, though: we learnt *money* and *Spanish* and *work*. We learnt that we had to work for money for needs we didn't have before; matches, salt and sugar. Why were we civilized? For what were we civilized? To be taught that we needed sugar and oil and money and clothes and food from the markets, more and more."

Tarzan stopped, angry and upset.

Another of the elders, Manuel, said, "we were scared of their white skin, and we were scared they would kill us. They did actually kill us. They brought illnesses *como un plago*, like a plague. These were illnesses we couldn't cure with plants. Six or seven thousand people got ill, and almost all of them died; influenza, fever, measles. The missionaries brought some medicine to cure the diseases they themselves had brought, but not enough." Here as elsewhere, when the local shamans couldn't cure these new diseases, their status was undermined. "We became embittered," said Tarzan.

I spoke to one Catholic priest in Harakmbut territory, to ask him about the arrival of the first missionaries. "We came like saviours and messiahs," he commented modestly. The people they "saved" told me a very different story. Within two years of missionaries establishing a base, fifty per cent of the local people were dead, killed by diseases the missionaries brought. When people first started dying of diseases brought by the whites, the deaths were blamed on female shamans and the Harakmbut killed the women. Jared Diamond remarks that the population decline among native people in the century or two following Columbus's arrival is thought to have been up to 95%. A holocaust.

W hile I was in Peru, several indigenous campaigners complained bitterly about missionaries. "They are responsible for the propagation of sicknesses and the annihilation of uncontacted indigenous people," they said and told me about one church in particular, whose practices were, well, evil is I think the right word.

One of their missionaries would take a high speed boat upriver, trying to trap the "uncontacted" tribes with biscuits and gifts, in spite of local indigenous campaigners trying to stop such deadly jaunts. It occured to me with a revolted curiosity, what kind of biscuits does he leave? Jammy dodgers? Ginger nuts?

In the forests around Cuzco, four Christian groups were competing with each other to reach the "uncontacted". I arrived in Cuzco on a Saturday night. Tomorrow, I thought, I would pay a visit to the Church of American head-hunters.

I talked to the pastor, who said he wanted to help uncontacted people co-operate with oil workers. "I think we should make a responsible contact," he said. "What's an irresponsible one?" I asked. "One that doesn't weigh the cost of contact, for example, medical needs," he replied suavely. But he was perfectly happy to bring diseases, I pointed out, which the local peoples' healers couldn't cure.

"We're too afraid of impinging on their culture," he said grandly—which frankly was not something I'd noticed. American culture needed to be respected just like any other, he said, and one part of its culture was to spread, to force itself on others. He pointed to a boy sitting next to me: "We cast twelve devils out of him three weeks ago," he said casually, as if he'd just unblocked the toilet.

The missionaries know full well that their contact can and does kill people; history tells them so, as well as campaigners. They know, too, that their arrival heralds the destruction of the wild forest itself, for missionaries will-ingly grease the path for logging and oil companies. Right-wing Christian fundamentalist groups are linked with the anti-environmental "Wise Use" movement in the States, both of which seek to attack wilderness conceptually and destroy it in actuality. They insist on playing their part in an ancient battle of implacable animosity between Christianity and the forest wildernesses. The sky-god versus the earth religions. The Church versus the pagans. The dark and tangly and sinful forests versus the light of the gospel, as the monks chopped down the deepest forests to bring actual and metaphoric light. And then there's sex.

• • •

The Christian god seems to be the only god in the entirety of world religions who doesn't fuck. No wonder he doesn't groove the groves, for the forests of the world are irrepressibly sexual places. The Wild Man of the woods is famously lustful, a hairy, half-naked creature, on the lurk for sexual encounters, with hot breath and a smoky look in his eyes. Pan, with capering goatish-ness and prolific masturbation, pings semen around the bosky woods, shagging the drunk maenads. Dionysus, god of having a wild time, was god of forest orgies, and the priapic Puck fucks everything in his grasp, lightfoot with reck-less fertility, and a restless, truculent horni-ness.

JUST MY PRESENCE HERE SHEDS LIGHT ON THIS MAN

Meanwhile in the Amazon, the Master of Animals is associated with the fertility of game, and rainbows represent his ejaculation. The Amazon, (like the forests of Europe used to do), throbs with an unmistakable pulse: the grinning green man, with a hooded wink, his green wand in one hand and his other–bolt upright–in the other.

Nature swells with sex, cooing, licking, flyting, courting, hinting, mating and intimating: carnal knowledge, knowing, kenning, cunning. Nothing unthrust. Nothing unfecund. Ripeness lusts till it rots, and its very rottenness makes a dank warm bed for the next tight tip to poke through. For, nudging deep down in the chthonic nub of things, in the sweet and musky smell of a warm rotting log, *eorthe* begins the cycle again.

The Christian church quite rightly identified wild nature with sex but then, in a cruel blow against life, decided to associate them both with the devil—fornicators were beasts and toads, the Devil was the Arch Beast. Pan was the personification of wild sex and the Christian church, quite horribly, identified Pan as Satan.

In West Papua, I met a missionary hell-bent on getting men to stop wearing penis gourds. In the Amazon I was told of missionary planes dropping cargoes of underpants. ("But they smelt funny, so we threw them in the river.") Sure-yani Poroso told me how the Leco people used to have sex outside, in the forests, up trees, by the river, in canoes, all over the place, but the missionaries came and insisted that people should only have sex enclosed, indoors, in bed, and in one position: the woman underneath. It was, of course, quite literally, the missionary position. "But no animal does it like two sticks. That was a law no one ever obeyed," said Sure-yani.

Bringing sex indoors was, I would argue, not so much to do with controlling sex between humans but rather controlling the sexual relationship between humans and nature. Because if that relationship was intimate and sensual—sexual even—then there would be no space for the Judaeo-Christian god. Only by prising human sexuality away from nature, only by claiming this sexuality was filthy, could you make space for Jehovah. This wild will of jungly sexuality was considered to be opposed to their god's will: in revenge, the god would come down on the Amazon like an almighty axe.

God's will could hardly have been clearer. Exodus 34 commands: "Ye shall... cut down their groves." Judges 6 commands the same. In the second book of Kings, chapter 18 sees Hezekiah cutting down the groves, while in chapter 23 Josiah is at it. The commandment of Deuteronomy 12 is that ye shall "burn their groves with fire." In the second book of Chronicles, chapter 14, Asa cut down the groves and by chapter 31, all of Israel cut down the groves. And just in case ye have not got ye message, Isaiah 17 stipulates that a man "shall not... respect... the groves."

The Boora people of the Peruvian Amazon called the first white man the "maker of axes" and the white world "the World of the Axe". They call a mestizo or European "the axe man," as they came to the Amazon, acting out the will of their axe god.

"We do not use the word environment," said a Yanomami man from Brazil. "That is your word for what is left of what you have destroyed." By 2011, there could be virtually no more tropical rainforest to save, warns one researcher.

The fundamentalist missionaries have axed not only the groves and lifeways of the forest but also the thoughtways, the philosophies, and knowledges of forest people. "The evangelical church extinguishes our knowledge, that richness," says a Shawi man in Peru. I met one Aguaruna shaman who was frightened to be known for what he was. He had good reasons. Ten to fifteen years previously, missionaries in this area persuaded the Aguaruna to think that their shamans were harming them, so the Aguaruna killed their own wisest men.

All over the Amazon, plants and trees are associated with knowledge. It's a universal understanding; the Buddha meditated under a tree, and sought wisdom from it. In India, Saddhus have always retreated to the forests for wisdom; and in traditional Indian thought, trees, in their previous lives, were great philosophers. The English language recognizes an association between wisdom and trees: an idea "takes root"; a book has "leaves"; a small book is a "leaflet"; you "branch out" into a new area of study. Christianity, like every other ancient system of thought, equated trees with knowledge, but–peculiarly–it chose to associate the Tree of Knowledge with sin. The woman is associated not with juicy life and regeneration but with evil. "Not enough cunt. That's the problem with Genesis," said one Ashaninca man to me.

Forest lore and shamanic knowledge is an entire way of knowing, as beautiful and profound as any in the West. A *curandero* is a qualified doctor, a shaman is a professor, a grove a university library. The Amazon has its artists, its John Clares, and its Mozarts, its Platos, Debussys and Ovids. Everywhere a depth of art and curing, music, metaphor and mind. The Amazon is a forest of knowing. But the fundamentalist sects, together with the corporations and States, have deforested the human mind.

So go on, then, pray, in your suburban housegroups and churches, pray for the Amazon and West Papua, in the name of god and capitalism, in the name of corpus christi and corporations, and I'll tell you what those prayers mean. The assault against nature is an assault against culture, hundreds of tribal cultures. This is what you pray for when you pray for the success of your missionaries. Go on, then, pray.

So kill pity. Crack down on kindness. Pour mercury over metaphor. Burn their books, hack down their languages and axe their philosophies. Tip Agent Orange into the eyes of a forest Picasso. Tie a Shakespeare's hands behind his back – with razorwire. Break Nureyev's ankles, stamp on Fonteyn's feet. Crack Joyce's head against a wall until the words whimper and fail him. Daub graffiti over an El Greco. Bulldoze the sculptures of Rodin. Burn the entire Oxford English Dictionary. Slash every copy of Dylan Thomas. Napalm the Berlin Philharmonic.

And where the forests used to ring with songlines and glow with knowing, praise your nasty little god and sing your fatuous Amen into the silent wastes. ☻

Jay Griffiths' new book, Wild: An Elemental Journey, *is published by Hamish Hamilton, price £20.*

The Futility of Protest

IS PROTESTING ABOUT WAR REALLY
WORTH THE EFFORT? BY TOM
HODGKINSON. ILLUSTRATIONS BY
HUGO TIMM

> War is over, if you want it
> — *John Lennon*

> The priest loves war, and the soldier peace
> — *William Blake*

> Every man thinks meanly of himself for not being a soldier
> — *Dr Johnson, in Boswell's* Life

There were 14 of us. We went down into the area of Oakland
where the violence was the worst a few blocks away from where
Huey Newton had killed that cop so we dealt with them when
they came upon us. We were well armed, and we had a shootout
that lasted an hour and a half. I will tell anybody that that was the
first experience of freedom that I had. I was free for an hour and
a half because during that time the repressive forces couldn't put
their hand on me because we were shooting it out with them for
an hour and a half. Three police officers got wounded. None of
them got killed; I got wounded. Another Panther got wounded.
> — *Black Panther Eldridge Cleaver, Interview, PBS, 1997*

> Bring me my bow of burning gold
> — *William Blake, Jerusualem*

THERE IS NOTHING so absurd as an anti-war protest. It's a war against a war, it's like going into the street and shouting "I hate words". They are tragically futile. Thousands march through the streets, saying, "oh, please!" to the government. The government peers out of its window and gazes down below, pleased that its actions are getting so much attention, but never for a millisecond diverted from its purpose. The anti-war protest is really one little pleasure that the liberal economy affords us: the opportunity to show each other that we are really nice people and hate killing. War provides us a with a fantastic excuse to get on our moral high horses. It is mostly, however, cant. And ineffective, too. When was the last time that a government changed its foreign policy as a result of a public protest? Please tell me.

The big surprise is that people even presume to show a sense of outrage and surprise when a government goes to war. Of course governments go to war! To be surprised when they do shows a fundamental misunderstanding of the nature of government. That is what they are there for. You voted for government and governments are warlike by nature. Therefore you cannot be surprised when Thatcher or Blair or anyone else goes to war.

Protest by its nature is negative. Take the experience of Permaculture gardener and *Idler* contributor Graham Burnett. Here he recalls his activist days:

Politicised by punk, my eyes were opened to the real world beyond school by Rock Against Racism. Shortly afterwards I became involved with animal rights groups such as the Hunt Saboteurs and various Anti Vivisection organisations. Throughout the eighties and up until the mid nineties I was a regular at meetings, pickets, protests and demonstrations: Ban the *Bomb, No Nuclear Power, Anti-Apartheid, No to the Poll Tax, Stop Clause 28, Boycott Shell, the Anti-McDonalds Campaign, Stop the Criminal Justice Act, No to GM crops and so on and on. Notice the pattern yet? Like so many radically motivated and socially concerned people across the progressive and "green" spectrums, my focus was on Stopping rather than Starting. Whilst protest and resistance movements are of course valuable and important, I had ended up defining myself more in negative terms of what I was Against rather than what I was positively For.*

This is all not to say that taking to the streets does not have its place and its use. It is certainly a pleasure in itself. It can also serve a useful communication purpose. It starts dialogue. It gets people together and it gets people talking. New ideas can come out of such gatherings. So I would never actually criticise the act of protest; it's just that it must be seen a mere beginning and not as an end in itself. Because practically speaking, marches in the street do not work. And as Chomsky says, what is the point? People go out on to the streets, wave banners around, feel good, think they've done their bit and then go back home. They switch on their tellies and start moaning again. Protest is not a mere diversion on a Saturday: it is an ongoing process, it should be part of everyday life, it requires constant effort.

Another form of protest might instead be to set a good example. Why don't the terrorists do this? Instead of killing people, they should be creating ideal Moslem communities in the UK so we can all see what a good religion it is. Graham Burnett, by the way, now runs vegetable and fruit gardens and produces magazines, books and websites which encourage others to take similarly freedom-seeking steps.

This is not to say that I am pro-war. Certainly I am not pro what war has become. But we have to ask ourselves whether the mechanised genocide pracrtised today is even worthy of the name war. Killing 600,000 Iraqis is not noble war with its own rules of combat. It is mere fearful mass murder, the act of cowards, mean bureaucracy. As is dropping nuclear bombs on people. Or any bombs. It is not war in the old noble sense of the word. It is cold, sterile killing. War used to have its own rules and was a sort of play, as Huizinga argues in *Homo Ludens*. The skirmishes and battles of medieval Europe were an expression of communal liberty: when Lucca attacked Florence, each state was affirming its freedom. And war and fighting was close up then; we had not delegated it to massive distant war machines. All cultures have traditions of noble warriors.

I seem to be intellectually against war, while wanting to preserve the noble ideals of knightly conduct, a confusing position to be in. I love to watch war films. The world loves *Star Wars*; it's our modern equivalent of the King Arthur legends, with Yoda as Merlin. I read stories of fighting and battle to my son Arthur. "Jack The Giant-Killer" is a favourite. Nowadays, we would not kill the giant, we would try to incorporate him into society and re-train him. It is a strange internal battle. I could never quite get my head around the way that my friend the late Gavin Hils, a committed pacifist, joined the Territorial Army. Some of his army colleagues came to his funeral and fine men they were. I would welcome suggestions from readers out there on how to reconcile my warlike impulses with my pacifist ones. And fighting is surely a sign of spirit. Penny Rimbaud asks the question: "what peace has been achieved without submission?"

Therefore, if we are not to bow under a certain authority then perhaps we have to fight it. This point was raised by John Wilkes in his famous North Briton No 45, the paper that was to make him world famous as a champion of freedom and which also got him thrown into the Tower. In it he attacked a recent speech by King George which called for a "spirit of concord" in the nation. He first criticised a recent invasion of civil liberties under which "private houses are now made liable to be entered and searched at pleasure":

A nation as sensible as the English, will see that a spirit of concord, when they are oppressed, means a tame submission to injury, and that a spirit of liberty ought to then arise, and I am sure ever will, in proportion to the weight of the grievance they feel.

Soldiers, too, are often admirable human beings. It is admirably brave to risk giving up your own life for the greater good. And whenever I meet a soldier, I find them to be an impressive breed of men: courteous, humble, capable, independent and non-materialistic. They have sought honour through self-sacrifice and are not motivated by money. And wouldn't you rather be a soldier than work in Dixon's? It is a far more intense life.

Children, boys anyway, seem to have an instinctive love of battle and contests. They positively revel in competitions of strength, agility, joke-telling. And most cultures keep games-playing alive into adulthood in one form or another. Contests of verbal dexterity, for example, is a Greek tradition which is today continued today by rappers. We test our knowledge and learning in pub quizzes. Game

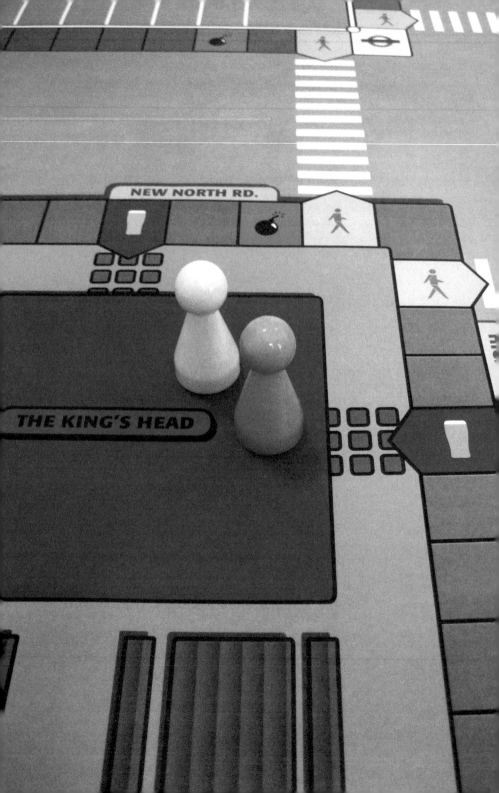

shows on TV also attest to the continuing instinct for showing off and matching our wits. And war is another contest, albeit a dangerous one. In fact, it is the opinion of the French writer Michel Tournier that it is not children who imitate men when they play at war; it is men who imitate their childish selves when they indulge in real war.

Now, when I first read Gandhi's autobiography, I was inspired. His work with the Untouchables was clearly helpful. His passive resistance idea, the calm nobility of turning the other cheek, seems laudable. But then I started thinking that perhaps, in actual fact, Gandhi was quite annoying. His smug vegetarianism, his chastity: he makes the rest of us look bad. His standards are too high. He didn't have the grand personality of a St Francis of Assisi; gone is the gay attire. Gandhi has a kind of Puritan austerity about him, refusing meat even when very ill. When Churchill called him a "half-naked fakir", it is an insult that is generally repeated in tones of great liberal shock and horror, at Churchill's racist brutality. But he was putting his finger on something, because in arriving in the UK half-naked, Gandhi appeared to be saying: "You are all idiots." Then there is Gandhi's famous comment about civilisation. But passive resistance is still resistance, it's just more annoying. It's morally superior resistance; it's trying to have your cake and eat it. The idler's way might be described as "active ignoring" or even "active acceptance", or perhaps "elegant sidestepping", to dance nimbly through life, clicking our heels at oppression, maybe that's the answer.

War anyway, can add intensity to life. In this sense it is playful. When a terrorist bomb struck London recently, my friend John Moore called me at my mother's flat in Shepherds Bush. "Pub?" he suggested. We decided to let the other suckers struggle in to work, which nowadays is painted as a gesture of defiance to the terrorists: "you may bomb us, but we'll carry on working and shopping." This is the message that is constantly blared out of radio stations on the day of such attacks. John and I decided to follow an alternative British tradition: the skive. So we enjoyed a very pleasant two hours in a pub on Kilburn High Road. All plans were off as no one knew what was going on. I had planned to travel home to Devon that evening but as the trains were ocancelled. There was no agenda. We went and had tea in John's garden and his neighbour called round. We enjoyed an oasis of pleasure in the now because who knew what was about to happen next. I thought that maybe this is what it might have been like for Londoners in the blitz, or indeed any war-time population. There was something thrilling and intense about the experience; you might as well enjoy yourself now because you might get blown up in five minutes.

And the Second World War led to a flowering of self-sufficiency: the nation was encouraged to grow vegetbales with the "Dig for Victory" campaign, and so there was a brief renaissance of a pre-industrial approach to food.

War is a game for boys. Let them play it but do not turn into a boy-man. War should be kept in the arena of play: jousts, competitions, horse-riding, war without tears, *jeux sans frontières* as that splendid TV programme used to have it. Or maybe we need to channel our warlike instincts into fighting oppression, like a Wilkes.

And as far as war at a national level goes, yes, comrades, the truly radical step is to make no resistance at all, and to go beyond the futile self-serving gestures of protest. Instead, create. 🌀

The
Original
Offence

UTOPIA AND PARADISE ARE VERY DIFFERENT IDEAS,
SAYS JOHN NICHOLSON

Breughel
"The Land of Cokaygne"
Bayerische Staatsgemäldesammlungen, Alte
Pinakothek Munich and Kunstdia-Archiv
Artothek, Weilheim, Germany

W

hat does the recurrent obsession with living in paradise tell us about calls for returning to Nature? Idling in paradise or utopia? Is the ideal state one of idleness or is idleness an ideal state? The garden of Eden or a man-made machine which manufactures happiness?

Every culture throughout history and all over the world has its paradise. Paradise is a natural state, for Christians remembered as a garden. The expulsion from Eden, the fall, the great lapse from grace, is the start of mankind's troubles. A return to the pre-lapsarian world has been a constant quest ever since. To return to innocence, to being one with God, is behind all calls for repentance and curses on civilization, especially as epitomised by city living. Attempts frequently require their practitioners to behave with the innocence of children or to shed artificial constructs even clothing and present themselves as naked Adamites.

In the Bible the first couple, thrown out of paradise, were forced to live on Earth. At once we realise that Eden, paradise, is self-contained and completely distinct, not related to Earth. Likewise Heaven was always the contradiction of Earth, not only the opposite of Hell. Some aspects of life on Earth could be heavenly or hellish but all three states were quite separate. We must also distinguish between heaven and paradise.

Examples of the desire to return to the simple natural life was expressed for the Romans by Virgil in the form of "pastoral". The shepherd was particularly favoured and Marlow wrote in the guise of one beseeching his mistress to live with him and be his love. His friend Ralegh responded with a realistic exposure of the chances. Arcadia is a theme through all Shakespeare's works.

But the tension between the dream and reality of paradise was finding more powerful forms of expression than lyrical poems. At the crucial turning point between Catholicism and Protestantism, between classicism and the Renaissance, an Englishman invented a new sort of paradise, one which might be realised on Earth. It is in the differences between paradise and utopia we can make out profound patterns.

Utopia is a joke. The Greek words mean "no place" or "now here/nowhere". (Paradise = everywhere.) The joke is not mine but Sir Thomas More's. More loved puns and that kind of word play. He had a vivid sense of fun. For instance we know he wore a hair shirt which made him bleed, scourged himself vigorously, expected his daughters to come naked to breakfast and was keen on dismembering offenders. Just the sort of man to invent an ideal world.

About a century after the Roman Catholic grandee's fall from grace his Anglican counterpart, Sir Francis Bacon, in forced retirement for corruption, wrote his recipe for the ideal society. More's first edition appeared in 1516 (the year Bosch died). Bacon's *The New Atlantis* was found among his papers after his death in 1626 and published the next year.

More developed his model society from Plato and from his Catholic faith. Platonic "guardians", grandees, would rule since they knew best. Regulated communities flourished in the many sacred houses and orders which would be dissolved by Henry VIII.

I stress the importance of the historical moment. Utopia appeared as England began to break from Rome and New Atlantis on the eve of the thirty years war to eradicate Protestantism. As warned, Anglicanism lead to more revolutions, not least in science. More heretical utopias appeared, almost a craze, such as Campanella's *City of the Sun.*

Bacon added scientific knowledge to the talents of his "guardians". His model society would enjoy the authority not only of divine and moral legitimacy but also of scientific certainty. It was logical that mechanical science would be invented in England.

These English ideal societies were theories of how man-made paradises on earth should be ordered. Here we arrive at a new idea: society must be re-arranged, ordered, on theoretical lines, in *this* world. Earth is to be re-made into a paradise. Both schemes rely on work. The citizens are defined by their roles as workers. Utopias have no place for slackers, criminals or opponents. Isn't utopia the guarantee everybody is well-adjusted? How to be out of step? Crime could not exist in communist states so the deviant element was not punished but re-educated.

Already we see many ways in which utopia differs from paradise.

For our purpose the main contrast is utopia's attitude to work. If work has a moral dimension so absence of work is wreathed in a negative aura. Not working is the opposite of resting, it is being lazy, idle. The citizen who does not fulfil the quota jeopardises the smooth-running of the social machine. The enemy of the people, the ultimate traitor.

Believers in the Gospel of Work see idleness leading to all sorts of vice and despair. To Nothing. To the eastern mind,

BOSCH, HIERONYMUS C. 1450 – 1516.
"THE GARDEN OF EARTHLY DELIGHTS"
LEFT HAND PANEL OF TRIPTYCH.
ON WOOD, 220 X 195CM.
MADRID, MUSEO DEL PRADO.
PHOTO: AKG-IMAGES

BOSCH, HIERONYMUS C. 1450 - 1516.
"THE GARDEN OF EARTHLY DELIGHTS"
MIDDLE PANEL OF TRIPTYCH. ON WOOD, 220 X 195CM.
MADRID, MUSEO DEL PRADO. PHOTO: AKG-IMAGES

Nothing is akin to nirvana, bliss, heaven. How different for the westerner who feels apocalyptic terrors since Nothing is staring into the pit. The void. Chaos. We unravel, our minds deliquesce, our identities merge, we lose self.

This epochal change in consciousness is the new inability to be still. Action is its own reward. A febrile energy expresses itself in a need to be forever active and exploring which, coupled with an inability to be unconscious of self, fuels missions to make a better world.

Do we find an imperative to be forever doing things in paradise? On the contrary! In paradise nobody worked. There is no need for punishment in paradise. No guilt, No shame. That is the entire point of paradise. In a way we could say paradise is based on the absence of obligation.

2

Mid way between Utopia and the New Atlantis a Flemish painter produced a version of paradise, "The Land of Cokaygne". The similarities between Breughel and Bosch are recognised but how about the differences?

Bosch's "Garden of Earthly Delights" attempted to make a visual account of paradise. Its title warned that the pleasures are of this world, not heaven. The painter reminds us we are not looking at paradise. Indeed the work is the centre panel of a triptych. The left panel shows the true paradise (the Garden of Eden) while the right side is hell. Bosch deliberately shows paradise as the garden of Eden in contrast to an Earthly paradise.

All three panels are entirely suffused by Christianity so paradise contains Adam and Eve with God. But the animals in Bosch's Eden are not all familiar species. They include monsters which, like the landscape, are fantastical and sinister. Birds and insects cross breed with fish. Creatures shape shift their bodies and their roles.

Paradise was a subject which Bosch painted frequently, at least six times. This one is revealing because it specifically contrasts Eden with a different earthly garden. In the middle of this version is one of Bosch's fountains. I call it a fountain but, although it is the centrepiece in the lake, it does not expel water. Not just its pink colour

but also its spikes and claw-like bits evoke shell fish, a sort of lobster. The earthly garden, the main panel, is full of such fountains, five of them, which replace the weird rock formations of Eden. The character of these constructs develops in this panel. All repeat the shell-like association but two project from globes, black and bomb like. Most of the fountains take on the nature of the rock formations of paradise and provide room inside.

The earthly garden is packed with incidents and allegories which there is no space to examine here. Look for yourself and find enough stories to fill a novel. There is plenty of kinky sexual incident for the bonk-buster market, indeed a veritable psychopathia sexualis. It doesn't take a genius to read some of the images. Any peasant could literally see what was shown; the allegory or metaphor was secondary.

A monstrous creature shoves a stiff human into its beak/mouth while shitting out a stream of bodies through a bubble into a hole. A chap pours puke into the hole so it is tasty. Somebody hangs their arse over the hole and shits coins into it. The body going into the beak has a flight of birds escaping from its arse. Arses are everywhere, making music or with roses sticking out while somebody whips with more roses.

Who can't recognise such situations? But the brilliance of Bosch is his ability to crystallise these episodes into images which are not only obvious on the surface but, equally obviously, contain deeper meanings. I suggest it is this code or visual language, coupled with the sexual atmosphere, which make the painting so popular and lasting.

Our purpose, however, is to distinguish

between the different worlds or states. Heaven is not the same as paradise. Heaven and hell, like paradise, are not of this Earth, unlike Bosch's garden. An earthly garden compared to paradise. There is also the matter of time. Christianity places paradise, Eden, at the beginning of the story while there is more than one ending. Heaven and hell are the product of the Last Judgement so both are after human death. There is a less remembered interval, limbo and the harrowing of hell when Christ goes into the devil's domain to rescue souls.

We have enough examples of Bosch's work to know he dealt in allegory. Breughel's picture belonged to the same tradition of proverbial images. This expects the viewer to "recognise" the meanings. Let's try.

In the foreground is a scene or episode. The landscape in the background is equally full of symbols. All increase the mood and bolster the story or message.

What are we being shown? "The Land of Cokaygne" is the name for the paradise of folklore. Neither the heaven of religious orthodoxy nor Eden. There are no divine beings. Cokaygne relates more to Arcadia than to the Garden of Eden but its central appeal is very different and suspect. The central action is inaction. Is there a better visual representation of the results of pleasure? Although there are earthly delights they are more obvious, less allegorical. Unlike Bosch's vision there is no hint of sex, only earthy urges. Is the Land of Cokaygne the state of bodily satisfaction? We are looking at three characters, completely zonked. They are not just asleep but, from the way their limbs are splayed, flattened by excess. They are sleeping it off. Before passing

out they had been feasting.

Feasting was a rare pastime. It had a timetable. The year was built around feast days because private banquets were unknown. Over-indulgence could only be communal, social. These three have been taking part in an act which was not forbidden as it was unthinkable. For only three people to revel meant they enjoyed unparalleled good fortune. This is confirmed by their surroundings. Food and drink are everywhere, accessible and inexhaustible.

The bulldogs all have rubber teeth,
The hens lay soft-boiled eggs.

We are in the Big Rock Candy Mountains.

O—the buzzing of the bees in the cigarette trees
round the soda water fountains
where the lemonade springs and the blue bird sings
in the Big Rock Candy Mountains.

The chorus is familiar but listen to the verses:

In the Big Rock Candy Mountains
You never change your socks,
And little streams of alcohol
Come a-trickling down the rocks.
The box cars are all empty,
And the railroad bulls are blind,
There's a lake of stew and whisky, too,
You can paddle all round 'em in a big canoe
In the Big Rock Candy Mountains.

The dream is to stop endlessly living on the run. No more toil. This could only appeal to people who work. It is not the idle poor nor the idle rich. There is no doubt we are in America. And hitching a ride for free. On the road, or rather on the railroad.

As supplies are inexhaustible in the Big Rock Candy Mountains so in the Land of Cokaygne. To reach the spot where they collapsed the three had to get through prairies of porridge. They crossed fences made of fat sausages and pigs running around with carving knives in their flesh ready to be sliced and eaten. This is the customary procedure. Geese also run about ready roasted. There is an egg with a spoon stuck in it for the languid. A tiny note of Bosch-like horror, this egg has legs to help it run to its consumer. Pancakes and tarts grow on the rooftops.

There is another strange aspect to the painting. The scene is cut off along the top. This effect is emphasised by the incredible tilting. The ground on which the three rest seems on the verge of sliding them off. Violent movement. So the puddings should slither off the roof.

Is there no gravity in Cokaygne? Or is movement frozen? There is plenty of action if we look. The food runs around but people just loll. They don't need to lift a finger. The knife may even unaided slice off the meat, as in a cartoon. So there is a kind of tension, frozen inaction, stillness, idleness. Although the three figures do not move, the world around them isn't still. Let us play with it. Will the egg and pig be in position when the men awaken? Do the food creatures, creature comforts, only move when nobody can see them? Is it all a dream? Are we looking at what the men are dreaming?

Goya's "The Sleep of Reason Produces Monsters" in usually interpreted to mean while Reason is asleep the weird reigns. My reading suggests otherwise, that Reason is a form of sleep in which we dream of grotesqueries. Therefore Reason is a state of monstrosities, not its antidote.

We are outdoors. But the atmosphere is claustrophobic because the top of the painting cuts off the vista. This is very important because this produces a perspective, a distance in the picture between the events in the foreground and background. We are looking at a representation of space which implicitly relates to movement. There is a movement, of our eyes. They move from the different scenes in different places. Although nothing in the picture moves the viewer moves.

3

Why is the world tilted at an angle in the Land of Cokaygne? Why is the top cut off to produce this closed-in atmosphere where gravity does not work and movement is frozen? Does The Land include the background or is the paradise enclosed in a normal world?

Today we take perspective in painting for granted but it is one of the main advances in civilization. The discovery of how to express perspective is seen as probably the greatest invention or change of consciousness we call the Renaissance or rebirth.

In simple terms perspective means how you see things. Viewing the world from unseen angles—like this article and the angled Land of Cokaygne. In its new sense perspective meant the co-existence of different dimensions. Clearly such a concept was revolutionary because it was previously unknown. But that did not prevent it being seen as the work of the devil.

Perhaps the best-known display of what could be done technically is 'The Betrothal of the Arnofini', 1434. Van Eyck translated the Italian invention to the Netherlands and he is called the first photographic painter. By the time of Breughel the techniques were commonplace. Recently fresh controversy has been caused by David Hockney's suggestions that paintings like this were done with camera devices. So what?

Playing around with perspective would be another huge change explored around the turn of the 20th century. Painters again provided the visual record but the entire school of modern Physics derives from such ideas. The Space-Time Continuum, the laws of thermo-nuclear dynamics, relativity—all are based on changes in perspective. If it is possible to see in 3D what about 4D? Psychedelic drugs had higher ambitions.

The public perspective about the differences between Modern art—now a century old—and traditional art usually revolve around this point. "True" art is realistic. It shows the real world, representing what our eyes see. It is like a photograph. At once we enter another maze. The camera could never lie and was expected to make painting redundant. The moving image, film, should do the same to photography. Then came colour... reality dissolves.

But it was all an illusion of reality.

Perspective was inseparable from the idea of trickery. The artist reproduced the real world, by *trompe l'oeil*, he tricked the eye. Using the arcane knowledge of mathematics and geometry, light and shadow, tones of colour, he simulated stone statues. He could make a flat surface look as though it was a frame through which the viewer was looking at a scene. A panel on a wall might appear as a window opening out on to a landscape and a bright sky.

EARLY PERSPECTIVE PAINTING WAS SEEN AS A
TROMPE L'OEIL TRICK

New sorts of paint were devised because they needed to be more flexible and slower drying. Slow and easy to move around. Oil-based paint had another benefit, it dried to a translucent surface which was softly luminous.

Not only was there an alternative reality but one which was full of movement. Domes spiralled up out of sight to the heavens, the ceiling. Symmetry gave way to the irregular, illusions and the bizarre combined in divine ecstasy. No wonder the Baroque would be known as "the Jesuit style" in defiance of heretical Protestantism.

As space could deceive so could time. In these paintings there was eternal daylight.

Our mind's eye can see what is now the traditional or customary perspective, the long view.

Now we understand that the tilting of planes relates to the conjuring trick which shows us other dimensions. No wonder this was thought to be black magic. Practitioners took their charges out of the visible world into a secret realm, or distorted reality to make it more real, heightened reality in the terminology. Passing through the doors of perception could bring you to heaven or hell. The drug allusions are no coincidence as altering how we see, perceive, lies at the core of the exercise. Perspective is like the effects of drugs, hallucinogens. We cheat and enter paradise by the side door, avoiding the Judgement.

4

Who are the revellers in the Land of Cokaygne? A soldier, a peasant and a clerk. Is this meant as an example of folly? How far from Bosch's divine cast. We see the tools of their trade, lying use-less. The peasant's flail is under his heavy prostrate body while the clerk has rolled up a document for a pillow. They couldn't work if they wanted to.

Are these three guilty of gluttony? That would be hard to prove. Are they guilty of sloth? There is no sign of that. Are they idle? Not possible. They are in a world where idleness has no meaning. Paradise.

To read the figures as sloth and gluttony misses the point of paradise. It may be there is a more hidden meaning which contradicts the assertion that this painting lacks contemporary allusions. Thought to have been done in 1567 it comes after another by Breughel showing a saint arousing his audience.

This refers to a campaign of sermons delivered in fields to crowds in the summer of 1566. These were intended to rouse Protestants to defend themselves against the Catholic threat. What was feared is plain in another picture "The Massacre of the Innocents" from the same year. Three or more years earlier had come "The Triumph of Death". In such a mood how would paradise play?

"The Land of Cokaygne" may belong to this sequence and show the results of a sleep of the selfish who live only for the pleasures of the belly. If the three are guilty of any offence could it be their feasting by themselves, not with the community? Consume in a selfish way and you endanger everybody else. You are consumed by an allegorical sleep. When they wake what prospect faces them? More feasting and more sleep. Is this paradise or a treadmill? "The Triumph of the Material". So the painting is not showing us the bliss of being idle or greedy. Like "The Garden of Earthly Delights", "The Land of Cokaygne" exists on Earth. Sur-

NATURAL MAN

Creator who worked a six-day week. Heaven, you may say, when forced to work at least forty hours a week. That show you how the work habit has taken hold. Who said you had to work regular hours anyhow? In a perfect society!

Utopia supplies lots of leisure activities. Sure, run by the authorities. Nothing you want to do for yourself. No ale houses or wine shops, no brothels, no blood sports or any of the activities so hated by the prigs. And the all-seeing eye checks that you aren't misbehaving, subverting perfection by idling.

For when we come to idling, utopias collapse. They are all orderly, even those with built-in variety. It is no accident the model society should become a subject of theory as the new work-ethic was born. Both stem from the same desire to mechanise the world and mankind. A factory run by robots is surely the ultimate utopia, one which abolishes humans.

How paradise was fucked is another story. The state of innocence would be turned into the "primitive" and re-discoveries of noble savages—or Darwinian missing links – abounded. Depends on your point of view.

The state of Nature replaced Eden, let alone the earthly garden. Delight stretched about as far as gender order or rubbing sticks together. Some spark. On the level of boy scouts when compared to Bosch, let alone Cokaygne. Red Indians were translated into Picts, our own "natives".

In this Progressive view the ancients not only built landscapes worthy of Bosch but also utopias which More would have admired.

How different from the home life of our own dear queen.

rounded by the terrorism of orthodoxy, paradise took on a new perspective.

If there is any validity in this reading we see how the struggle of the new consciousness altered the traditional love of paradise. Sixty years later *The New Atlantis* developed utopia in its scorn for idleness.

You might imagine the perfect world was one in which you don't need to earn a living, where work is voluntary, a pleasure. Yet we already find this is not how the inventors of utopia think. They see work as a value, a good in its own right. They think everybody should be busy, always active, never lazy.

In More's utopia the number of hours citizens were required to work is a six hour day. More is nearer to the Euro working week. There is an echo of the

Idle Idol:

Charles Bukowski

THE POET WHO SUNG THE PLEASURES OF DOING BUGGER ALL. BY MARCUS O'DAIR

Over a decade after his death, Charles Bukowski is regarded as one of the most important figures in twentieth century American literature. He is also a hero to generations of slackers the world over, thanks to both his constant war on the nine-to-five world and its accompanying wage-slave mentality, and his celebration of such idle pleasures as wildly excessive drinking, pissing away huge chunks of time at the racetrack and retiring to bed for periods of three or four days at a time.

Admittedly, much of his public perception derives from the antics of his literary alter ego, Henry Chinaski, a persona that involved a fair bit of exaggeration. Yet the main themes in the work are certainly shared by the real-life Bukowski, not least of which is the vital importance of doing bugger all.

"This is very important–to take leisure time," he told his friend Sean Penn in 1987. "Pace is the essence. Without stopping entirely and doing nothing at all for great periods, you're gonna lose everything. Whether you're an actor, anything, a housewife, there has to be great pauses between highs, where you do nothing at all. You just lay on a bed and stare at the ceiling. And I don't mean having profound thoughts. I mean having no thoughts at all. Without thoughts of prog-ress, without any self-thoughts of trying to further yourself. Just... like a slug."

Largely uninterested in material possessions, Bukowski's disregard for money was such that, according to biographer Barry Miles, he would forget to pick up his paychecks for anything up to a month, much to the annoyance of his fellow employees who were desperately counting down the days for each one.

This attitude locates him well and truly on the idler's side of the all-important money-versus-time equation and, combined with his preference for slug-like slackerdom, it is no surprise that resentment towards work became the main theme in his writing (alongside drinking, naturally). The following conversation between Bukowski and his boss, for instance, is taken from the novel *Factotum*:

"Chinaski, you haven't been pulling your weight for a month and you know it."

"A guy busts his damned ass and you don't appreciate it."

"You haven't been busting your ass, Chinaski."

I stared down at my shoes for some time. I didn't know what to say. Then I looked at him. "I've given you my time. It's all I've got to give–it's all any man has. And for a pitiful buck and a quarter an hour... so that you can live in your big house on the hill and have all

ENEMY OF THE NINE-TO-FIVE

the things that go with it. If anybody has lost anything on this deal, I've been the loser. Do you understand?"

The fact that he "always started a job with the feeling that pretty soon I'd quit or be fired" meant that he never got sucked into thinking about anything silly like career prospects. Instead, his main aim at work was "to wonder about doing nothing, always avoiding the boss and avoiding the stoolies who might report to the boss."

His absenteeism, too, is the stuff of legend, seeing him fired from job after job, and even during his major period of sustained employment, a twelve-year stint at the post office, Bukowski's attendance was so outrageously poor that it was allegedly the subject of an FBI investigation

(alongside his "obscene writings" in the underground press).

So strong was Bukowski's opposition to the nine-to-five–which he described variously as "one of the greatest atrocities sprung upon mankind", "the sickest of all sick things", and, quite seriously, "worse than death"–that some have interpreted his work as socialist or even anarchist. Pointing to Orwell's acknowledged influence, Howard Sounes, another biographer, describes some of Bukowski's writing as "virtually a polemic against capitalism", although the man himself always insisted that his writing was apolitical.

Still, whether part of a political agenda or simply a personal philosophy, it's pretty clear that Bukowski wasn't the biggest fan of the eight-hour day. Ironically, however, his oft-cited lack of ambition meant that he himself did not leave this hated world until the grand old age of 49, despite his long-held view, as expressed in Post Office, that: "any damn fool can beg up some kind of job; it takes a wise man to make it without working".

Ultimately, of course, he would achieve this goal through writing, but the man who Jean-Paul Sartre called America's greatest living poet would first spend many years lazing around getting drunk and working in dead-end jobs for something like $1.80 an hour.

Initially, his only practical attempt to escape from the stream of what were, in idle parlance, crap jobs, was not through writing but gambling. While many assumed that his love of the racetrack was down to plain old enjoyment, in fact Bukowski hated crowds and "didn't give a fuck about horses"–the appeal, quite simply, was that "in one six furlong race, say in a minute and nine seconds, you make a month's pay".

Of course, backing a winner was far from guaranteed, but, as he told the *Los Angeles Free Press*, the idler in him could not resist even the possibility of easy money: "I piss away so much time and money at the racetrack because I am hoping to make enough money so I will not have to work any longer in slaughterhouses, in post offices, at docks, in factories."

Eventually, however, Bukowski found a more successful way to "make it without working", finally taking the leap into full-time writing following the guarantee of $100 a month for life from John Martin of the Black Sparrow Press.

True, strictly speaking this was still work, as Bukowski himself acknowledged in *Upon The Mathematics Of The Breath And The Way*: "Writing, finally, becomes work if you are trying to pay the rent and child support with it. But it is the finest work

and the only work, and it's a work that boosts your ability to live and your ability to live pays you back with your ability to create."

And his particular method of writing was less taxing than most: in the same piece, he replies to the accusation that he'd be a great writer if he put in more effort with a great quote from Wallace Stevens: "success as the result of industry is a peasant's ideal."

The idea that the process of writing should not require effort pops up again and again, the following example being plucked from a letter to Gerald Locklin: "Writing has always been a pleasure to me, a non-work item, it's as easy as drinking so I usually do them both together. I hear from other writers how HARD it is to write and if it were that god damned hard for me, I'd try something different."

He wrote spontaneously ("I never liked hard work. Planning is hard work") and revised little ("I'm lazy"), and his style, influenced by Hemingway and Fante, was deliberately straightforward; genius, he once suggested, "could be the ability to say profound things in a simple way".

Inertia governed not only the style of writing and the writing process itself, but also what happened to the writing once it was completed: Bukowski simply sent John Martin everything he wrote, giving him carte blanche to print or reject as he saw fit, then passed the cast-offs to other publishers.

All of this goes a long way to support Neil Gordon's assertion, printed in the *Boston Review*, that there was "probably no literary figure in America who has done less to promote himself." True, Bukowski became hugely respected within the literary community and well known to the general public both in the United Stated and Europe, but there is a real sense that he achieved this position almost by accident.

Certainly, there were limits to Bukowski's indolence and, inevitably, there are certain anomalies that don't quite fit the idler interpretation of his life and work. Though it may not be evident in his books, Bukowski had a self-confessed Puritan streak and, as Barry Miles points out, "contrary to his public image, he was rarely unemployed for long and some of his jobs he held down for years, even during the so-called 'ten-year drunk'."

Further, contradicting Miles' story about him failing to collect paychecks, Howard Sounes describes the supposedly insouciant writer as "essentially conservative when it came to money". Sounes links this directly to Bukowski's alarmingly high work-rate: he wrote *Post Office*, his first novel, in just three weeks "but did not reward himself with a break—quite the contrary, he felt compelled to write almost constantly, partly because he was terrified of not earning enough to support himself."

Ultimately, however, Bukowski's place as icon of idling is surely beyond dispute. A recurring theme in the Barry Miles biography is that of Bukowski as "a fritterer away of time, a loiterer... the epitome of the French *flaneur*", which automatically places him near the very top of the idling hierarchy.

Such a view is supported by Bukowski's biographic details, his vitriolic attacks on the nine-to-five and even his writing style itself, all of which add up to a picture of a man who values his time and simple pleasures above all else.

Towards the end of his life, he was still ranting against "the eight-hour job, the payments on the car, the TV programmes, the movies, saving to send Jimmy to college," this time in *Portfolio* magazine. He continued: "Most people are dead long before they are buried, that is why funerals are so sad. Most people have missed everything: the fine paintings, the good books, the great classical symphonies. They believe that survival consists of commercial success... Happiness and meaning in life are not constants but I do believe at times we can have both if we can arrange to sometimes do what we want to do, what we truly feel like doing, instead of following pre-set rules. It's all quite simple—and worth fighting for."

For a more succinct motto, and for the ultimate evidence of Mr Charles Bukowski as idler extraordinaire, we need look no further than the man's gravestone, upon which are engraved just two simple words: "Don't Try". ◉

Bukowski was born in Germany in 1920, although he was brought up in Los Angeles where he spent the majority of his life. In 1955 he nearly died from an alcohol-induced ulcer, yet, despite ignoring medical advice to abandon drinking, he lived until the age of 73, eventually dying of leukemia.

With a prolific output of novels, short stores, poems and even a screenplay, Bukowski's bibliography can appear a little daunting to the newcomer. Post Office*, his first and probably best novel, is as good a place as any to start, followed by* Ham On Rye *and possibly* Factotum*. For short stories,* Hot Water Music *and* Tales Of Ordinary Madness *are hard to beat, while key poetry collections include* The Last Night Of The Earth, You Get So Alone Sometimes That It Just Makes Sense*, and* The Days Run Away Like Wild Horses Over The Hills*. Particularly recommended for idlers at the poems* Life Of A Bum *and* Something For the Touts, The Nuns, The Grocery Clerks And You.

Citizen Steere

THE LATE SIXTEENTH CENTURY IN BRITAIN SAW
THE BEGINNINGS OF TODAY'S WORK ETHIC AND
MONEY WORSHIP. BARTHOLOMEW STEERE WAS
KILLED BY THE STATE FOR EXPRESSING HIS DOUBTS
ABOUT THE NEW FAITH. BY JUSTIN POLLARD,
ILLUSTRATIONS BY ANKE WECKMANN

The official history of Britain doesn't contain a lot of protest. I suppose there's the Peasants' Revolt and the Civil War but after both of those we generally went back to exactly what we had before–why change things? But just below the level of BIG history there are quite a few complaints–we just don't often hear about them. Perhaps they interfere with the splendidly comforting image of the ship of British State sailing into a glorious future with all hands proudly working at their correct station. Or perhaps we just like our history to appear to be going somewhere in an orderly fashion.

And in truth what the hell have we got to complain about? Life has always been pretty good in the old "green and pleasant" hasn't it? Well, apart from the Black Death then. Take the sixteenth century–what a great time. Holbein painting lovely pictures of fat, jolly kings, Shakespeare writing splendid plays about mad Danish monarchs, the Spanish Armada, people shouting "Hey Nonney Nonney" just for fun, Gloriana and everyone returning home at the end of the day to a home grown, home cooked fully organic meal enjoyed in a pastoral idyll. What a brilliant time to be alive.

Actually that all depends on who you were really. For the sort of people who owned metal hats with jewels in them it wasn't a bad century at all–few centuries are–but for many, perhaps most, of the people of Britain it was, perhaps, one of the worst centuries to live in. Bizarrely we just refuse to talk about it. Perhaps that's because it's the century that set us on the path to our modern lives with its Protestant work ethic, belief that idleness is next to evilness and conviction that earning money is the only

really suitable way to spend the time. Take the case of poor old Bartholomew Steere.

One night in the autumn of 1596 Bartholomew Steere climbed Enslow Hill near Bletchingdon in North Oxfordshire, and not because he wished to savour the bucolic scene below but because he wanted to start a revolution. He'd been preparing for several weeks and talked to a lot of the local people, particularly those like him: the young men whose families had been peasant farmers in this area and the servants in the big houses for centuries before. He was angry—they all were—because the life they'd been sold was a lie and he intended to do something about it. He'd asked his supporters to go round the villages finding like-minded souls and arranged a rendezvous that night on Enslow Hill—that was where the people of North Oxfordshire would gather and the next day that was where the revolution would begin.

And so the sun sunk down and the first of the rebels began to arrive—ten men and boys variously armed with a selection of antique pikes, one rather fetching rusty sword and a dog. On top of the hill they gathered and lit a fire and waited for the people of Hampton Gay and Hampton Poyle and the staff from the great houses to swarm out of their homes and come to join them.

The next morning brought a scene none of them had been expecting. There, arraigned on Enslow Hill were—ten men, a handful of pikes, one rusty sword and a dog. No one else had come. So they put the fire out and all went home. The North Oxfordshire Rising was over.

So what had our young firebrand Bartholomew hoped to achieve if he had managed a better turn out? Well he didn't want a real revolution. He was quite happy with old Queen Bess doing her Gloriana bit. He didn't even want a better job, or one of those metal hats. What he wanted was a life like his father's. That wasn't a particularly exciting sort of a life but it had its moments. His family were farmers who rented land from the local landowner and worked it to grow the food they needed for their family and, in good years, something extra to sell to pay for those little luxuries–like shoes. It was a life regulated by the church, which provided the feast days and holidays (quite a few of them) that marked out the staging posts of the year and provided a safety net for those who were too ill or old to work. Not the most stunning remuneration package perhaps but a regular one. And one that Bartholomew Steere couldn't have.

Traditionally a young man like Bartholomew would need some land to start his own independent life. He might be given a plot by his family, if they could spare it, or he might do some wage labour to get the money together to rent his own patch. With a bit of land he could then build a house and then he'd be an eligible bachelor and stood a chance of finding a wife. And so, in the normal course of things, a new generation of little Steeres would appear on the scene and repeat the above.

But this wasn't going to happen to Bartholomew. A new entrepreneurial age was dawning and landlords were realising that there was a lot more money to be made turning over their lands to sheep pasture than collecting meagre rents off a bunch of peasants. So they began enclosing their fields and kicking their farmers out. Sir Thomas More, who found the whole thing rather disturbing, put it like this: *your sheep that were wont to be so meek and tame, and so small eaters, now, as I hear say, be become so great devourers and so wild, that they eat up, and swallow down the very men themselves.* And that's just what was happening to the people of North Oxfordshire–they were being eaten by sheep, metaphorically speaking. So what was Bartholomew to do? How about a job in the new sheep farming business with the now much richer landlord? Nope. Sheep farming requires a lot less manpower than growing crops. Apart from a shepherd or two, the landlord had no need for all these inconvenient people who had lived on his land. How about moving elsewhere? Well quite a lot of people were trying that and a lot of places were becoming decidedly unwelcoming. In 1570 the good burghers of Norwich had made a census to discover just how many of these dispossessed people had moved to the city and were horrified to find that even the abandoned towers of the old medieval wall were now crammed with what they rather charmingly referred to as the "*miserable poore*". They certainly didn't want any more.

What about new types of job? There were openings appearing, although not yet in any real numbers, in the wonderful world of factory work. These were still mainly confined to the woollen industry in East Anglia where, for a few lucky people, subsistence farming with its relatively high numbers of days off and small degree of independence was being replaced by relentless, grinding wage-labour. But even if Bartholomew could have faced the change in lifestyle there wasn't a place for him in the factories yet.

Hmmmmm. Tricky. Well then the State would have to provide surely. Er, No. Traditionally, the church had provided for the poor and dispossessed in each parish. In fact, in the mediaeval period the really painfully poor had provided something of a service to the rich. Providing alms was important for any wealthy person hoping to make a reasonably speedy passage through purgatory and into eternal bliss. It was a pleasingly simple system—pay for the poor, the poor pray for your soul, God takes a look and agrees this is all absolutely splendid and the Pearly Gates swing wide. Well that's a slight simplification, but you get the idea.

But the medieval church had been swept away in the Reformation. Protestants didn't believe in purgatory and local church charities were being wound up. The monasteries had all gone as well in the Dissolution, taking with them the alms they had traditionally provided. There was nowhere for Bartholomew Steere to go and no one to provide for him. Not that he would need looking after for much longer.

The North Oxfordshire Uprising might have been a bit of a damp squib but the official response to it was not. Bartholomew and his friends probably would have got away with what was, after all, in reality nothing more dangerous than a slightly unpopular picnic, had it not been for a local vicar with a broken bookshelf. He had called in the local carpenter Roger Symonds from Hampton Gay to mend it and, as he did just that, he chatted in the way that workmen are wont to do. And the conversation went something like this:

Carpenter: Hear about them revolutionaries on Enslow Hill the other night?

Vicar: No?

Carpenter: Said they were going to cut the throats of all the toffs.

Vicar: Bugger.

The result of this little tête-à-tête was absolute mayhem. Panic spread around the enclosing landowners and many took to their beds for weeks feigning illness in the belief that the roads were now filled with cut-throat peasants baying for their blood. News also spread to London where the Government was getting a bit nervous about all the rural poor who had nowhere to go and nothing to do. They dispatched a man to Hampton Gay to interview the carpenter who reported that Bartholomew had been going round town saying:

[I] care not for work, for we shall have a merrier world shortly; there be lusty fellows abroad, and I will get more, and I will work one day and play the other.

Warrants were immediately sent out for the arrest of the "ring-leaders" and four men, including Bartholomew Steere were captured. So fearful was the government that the nation was on the brink of some brilliantly engineered peasants' revolt that specific orders were sent saying how the men should be lashed to horses for the journey to London to prevent them talking to each other or getting word to their fellow conspirators and effecting a rescue. They needn't have bothered and Bartholomew and his friends arrived in London for their trial without incident.

Before trying them they were "softened up", torture being officially sanctioned here for one of the last times in British history, and this saved the hangman a job, at least in Bartholomew's case. He and one of his friends both died under interrogation. The other two were set before their judges and duly sentenced. Both were then taken back to Enslow Hill where they were hanged, drawn and quartered. And so another great British protest movement was swept under the carpet. Well, had you heard of Bartholomew Steere before today?

But the North Oxfordshire Rising should be remembered and celebrated. It was an idler's revolution if ever there was one. It set out to question why "progress" had to be considered good regardless of the consequences, it queried why life should be measured simply in terms of work and it doubted whether wealth was really the only measure of success. The sixteenth century was a great success for the landowners of North Oxfordshire but if we agree that it was a century of progress then we must applaud the people who dragged Bartholomew Steere to his death. He represented something new and scary, something to be stamped out – the idle poor. Not that Bartholomew intended to spend all his days in idleness. He just wanted to run his own life and have the occasional day off – a vision of heaven blinkered by his own grinding poverty. And if that's too much to ask then I for one, protest. ☺

News From Nowhere

HIDDEN IN THE HILLS OF SOUTHERN SPAIN LIES A
UTOPIAN VILLAGE, AN EXPERIMENT IN COMMUNAL
LIVING. MISHKA HENNER WENT THERE AND
BROUGHT BACK THESE PHOTOS

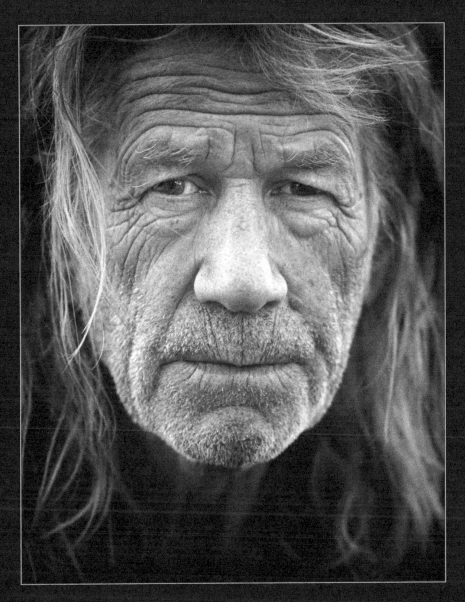

THE CONVENIENCES
of
PHILOSOPHY

PENNY RIMBAUD

PART ONE – THE MEANING OF LIFE

"We are effectively destroying ourselves with violence masquerading as love."
R.D. Laing

What is the meaning of life? Being a question which has been asked throughout time, or at least since the Athenian élite abandoned the spirit and took to the bottle, it presupposes a meaninglessness which has been the bane of Western philosophy. Essentially self-negating, the question quite simply is the answer. In any case, why *should* life have a meaning? Regardless of how we might choose to see it, life just gets on with itself, being what it is, leaving no question to be asked. On the other hand, if life has no meaning, then asking the question only confirms the implication made by it, indeed goes further in creating a temporal *fact* of meaninglessness.

> **The intellect is a defiler.**
> **The tarn lays dark and still.**
> **There is moss and cotton-grass.**
> **Sitting upon the thermals,**
> **the chough rises to great heights:**
> **the intellect is a defiler.**

However intellectually astute or philosophically reasoned, it is the pronouncer who makes the pronouncement, and that alone excludes any reason but her/his own. *"God is dead. I'll just slip into something more comfortable."* No one's talking to anyone but themselves. Like the clothes we dress ourselves up in, philosophical statements are subject to the whim of the moment, employed not as isolated observations, but to justify a current state of mind, a means, albeit temporarily, to harness our unimpressible, deeper, authentic being: a means to an end, our end.

"Do you love me, Ronnie?"

Just as the doing is in the act, so the statement: the point is not in the word, but in wordless intention. As we move through the consensual construct of linear time, so we describe ourselves within it. How else might we know we exist? In which case, what is philosophy but mere convenience, a retreat from the profoundly glorious chaos from which we were snatched at birth, but which nonetheless remains our birthright? Born from and into nothingness, we are force-fed the sour milk of human kindness that we too might suffer a life of enclosure. It is the trinity of family, church and State that conspire together in this repeated destruction of human will. There is no escape. Like the three monkeys, we are rendered deaf, dumb and blind in a world burgeoning with joy, and this is the person who we grow to accept as ourselves.

> **Philosophy is a clock-tower.**
> **I am exploded, yet contained,**
> **a vessel seeking order where there**
> **is no order and no vessel.**
> **The peach tree is laden with fruit:**
> **apricot, grape, mango.**
> **Philosophy is a clock-tower.**

Jill feels empty this morning, but that's nothing new. The coffee fails to awaken her senses. Jack has already left for work. She feels unfulfilled. She can't remember when they last made love. She's worried about Jack, but doesn't really know why. Is he having an affair? There's no reason for her to imagine that he is, but men of his age often do, so that's good enough reason, in any case, doubt is a better form of connection than none at all.

She remembers that she's got to pick up the holiday snaps from Easy Print. That should be interesting.

"Nice one, nice." The call of the psychic executioner. *"Hold it right there."* The past is an illusion, a singularly flimsy construct serving to prove a time and a place which never existed. It's not a case of *"was it really like that?"* as much as *"what is it?"* or *"is it at all?"* "It" in this instance being a technologically-trapped moment pertinent not to the moment, but to the technology. Does the clock tell the time or time tell the clock? The reflection is not the being, the shadow not the form.

"There's a place for us, a time and a place for us, hold my hand and I'll take you there."

DIRTY-ONE AND STILL COUNTING. CHERNOBYL, APRIL 1986:
thirty-one dead, many more to die through long-term effects of radiation.

Just as clocks confirm and compound the construct of linear time, so, in defiance of modern physics, photography confirms the construct of linear space: past, present and future. The power of Hollywood and Hello magazine are in their perpetuation of the renaissance conceit of "I the observer" (the fly on the wall), against the framelessness suggested by Einstein's relativity and Picasso's cubism (the fly in the ointment): order at all costs. By the middle of the twenty-first century, expect to be reading decimal time: the ten hour clock. No variable. It's the only way forward, the American way: determined, linear, monovisioned. *"The real thing."* Fine, but where do we exist in all this? There is no common answer because, beyond semantics, common answers are structurally impossible.

There are no "real" things
@
www.onoffyesno.com

"Hold my hand and we're halfway there."

THE SOUND OF ONE HAND CLAPPING:
fusion reactions are responsible for starlight and the operation of the hydrogen bomb.

I study a snapshot of someone who I am told was me. It's a schoolboy, maybe twelve years old. He's grinning, and he'll grin for evermore: grainy, grey and wretched. I feel a wrench in my belly. The primal pool is being disturbed. The knots are forming.

> "Jack does not see something.
> Jill thinks Jack does see it.
> Jack thinks Jack does see and Jill does not.
> Jill does not see herself what
>   she thinks Jack does see."
>   "Knots" R.D. Laing

This snapshot is not me. It is not what I was, nor what I have become. As much as I am now a self-fiction, an ornamental surface upon the existential void, so that grinning schoolboy is designed to establish the idea of consensual form as de facto. In my case he cannot succeed, for I am neither the he nor the me who sees him.

Jack glances at his watch. Firstly it's a Rolex Oyster, secondly, and less importantly, it's ten-thirty. He hasn't looked up all day. He notices a rash on the back of his hand. Maybe it's a melanoma. Unwisely if it is, he scratches it. He's supposed to be filing an insurance claim on behalf of Jill, in fact he's committed to doing so, but just at the moment he wants nothing of it. The computer screen is in idle mode. There's multi-coloured fish drifting across his retina, a migrainal mælstrom, but he's only dimly aware of its existence. The luminosity loans a lurid hue to his rash.

CUSTOMER ANNOUNCEMENT:
"the ten-fifteen to Tyneside is running as normal, it's just not showing up on the screen."

If there is an absolute, which by any reasoning there must be, then the absolute is not just the all, but the only, in which case, we cannot be removed. How, then, is it that we feel so removed? Is it, in fact, that we are mass in constant flux, confused only by the psychic limitations of self-enclosure?

I fearlessly throw myself
into the unknown
knowing that I am protected
by my own fear.

Jill had suffered neck and facial injuries in the accident. As the taxi zigzagged its way up the mountainside, Jack and Jill had been watching their hotel on the beach shrink from view. *"Next year?" "Oh yes, yes."* The taxi-driver had been looking up Jill's skirt through the rear-view mirror. The donkey just happened to be crossing the road. Jack thinks Jill has never been the same since, only he doesn't really think about it any more; to Jack it's become an insurance form supported by a doctor's certificate, and so has she. They haven't fucked since god knows when.

"Oh well, that's life."

What life? If we are a part of it, how can it be described as an experience separate from ourselves? Likewise, if we are apart from it, how can it be perceived as anything but idea dressed in the ragged cloaks of our own prejudices and conceits? Part of it or apart from it, life cannot be experienced as itself for it is just that, itself, and nothing more. We don't even enter into the equation.

$$E = me^2$$

Seeing ourselves within the psychological framework defined by misanthropists such as Freud, rather than directly
                            experiencing life,
we watch ourselves experiencing it
as a separate entity:
            the experience of
            experiencing
            experience.

Like Narcissus, we are in love with our own reflection, always once removed, always existing outside and beyond our deeper authentic being. The great passion of our emotional field has become so bastardised and enclosed by Freudian inhibition that we are bereft, mere flotsam incapable of engaging with the righteous storms of life-giving consciousness. In short, we have ceased to exist.

I
AM
NOT
THEREFORE I
BUY
I BUY THEREFORE I AM.

Within commodity culture, existence is expressed through individuality, which in turn is expressed through consumerism: you are what you buy, *"Just Do It."* But do what? Following the edicts of retail therapy gurus, be it fashion by Armani or lifestyle by Barefoot Doctor, we invest in an idea of ourselves, banking on others seeing us as we want to see ourselves. This is not individuality, but a chronic case of social schizophrenia where the dialogue between the authentic and inauthentic being has become so confused that consensual standards become the only ones to turn to. In this sense it is not God who is dead, but ourselves. We have returned to the swamp and buried our existential self.

"The Emperor is in his altogether..."
Nietzsche

Jill phones through to Jack at the office. *"Can you pick up the snaps?"* It's not actually a question, it's an order. She doesn't know that, but Jack's irritation indicates that he does. It's ten-thirty-five.

**Conflict is by nature both
self-realising and self-perpetuated;
it cannot exist without you.
THEN WHY CREATE IT?**

Jack is feeling sexually frustrated. Jill is his whipping post. *"She never really loved me anyway."* Jack is unconsciously involved in an act of psychic murder, posing the question *"what is love?"* For the answer, he needs look no further than his own containment.

**Rather than the "nouning" fate
of psychic suffocation,
the pain exquisite of love and hate
is the "verbing" cusp of illumination.
The light-switch is never far away.**

Jill seems to be staring out of the kitchen window. Her hands dangle limply in the tepid waters of the sink. In truth, her focus is fixed on the smudged glass of the window and she's not looking at anything at all. Whereas she thinks she's thinking of Jack, she is in fact thinking of nothing at all. Since the accident she's been cold inside, it's as if something has died in her. Her facial scars are like a yearning, tight and pulling like the call of the beach, distant, fading. Jill is on a drift. If she was able to feel anything at this moment, it would be misery.

Our understanding of life and death is not just limited by our self, it is utterly confined by it. We are the creator and the creation. We alone define our own condition. We are an (as yet) unavoidable act of enclosure. The world which we inhabit is nothing but a set of attitudes, our own attitudes, paradoxically both single and divorced: a self-imploding, negative duality. Call it reality if you will, but it is your reality and yours alone. How, then, if we are so totally enclosed, can there be so much interpersonal conflict. Yours?   Mine?

**The Twin Towers were there by design.
Jesus died for his own sins,
not mine.**

There is only one voice, one thought; yours. There quite simply is no argument but your own. Accept that, and you're halfway down the path to enlightenment. Reject it, and you are both killer and noose.

**LET THE BLOOD FLOW.
LET THE TRAPDOOR OPEN.**

"Bastard." A call from nowhere. Jill is unconsciously involved in an act of psychic murder. Jack dangles three-foot above a shit-stained York-stone floor, dancing the dance of chitter-chat.

Debate within the consensual is
              nothing but collusion.
Left?   Right?
              They're both dead
                   centre,
              every bit as self-deluding
         as the smiling Buddha's middle way.
Yin,   yang?
         Who are we trying to convince?
                There are no sides.
         Global war is a personal matter,
                strictly internal.
You make it,   you break it.
                Either way,
         the washing-up still needs doing.

Jill's fingers twitch involuntarily, knocking together two coffee cups. She hears the bells ring and looks down surprised. One of the cups has lipstick marks. It isn't her cup.

"Bastard."
**The past is just a fantasy,
just another way of saying *"me, me, me."***

As much as I am construct now, so I am as a grinning schoolboy. Time's span is just another case of consensual spam. Here's the myth surrounding the photograph. The day it was taken, I was caned for wearing luminous socks to school and informed that I should remember that I was not a teddy boy, but a public school boy, and that that carried responsibilities. After having been caned, I was sent home to change into something appropriate, which I knew to be as uniform and grey as the life planned ahead for me. My mother cried, not because of the burning welts on my arse, but because of the shame I had brought into her life. The welts were as lurid as the socks which had been their cause. Both were expressions of someone who I already knew was not me.

I was not, and am not, my mother's son.

When Jack and Jill were away, Jill would sit in the shade of the taverna, sipping a mango smoothy, watching Jack taking his morning swim; right out to the furthest buoy and back again, regular as clockwork. He always seemed very pleased with himself, the kind of pleased which made her feel she was being criticised. It was a daily ritual.

[NOTE] There's a wind blown up across the lake, giving the air a sulphurous tang. I am told that the lake is bottomless, but I'm not convinced. It doesn't make sense. I'm also told that fish can't survive in these waters. That makes a little more sense. The only thing which appears truly bottomless is the sky, but that's above me, so I guess it must be topless. One thing's for certain, there's not a fish any of us know of that can survive in the sky.

Sometimes after Jack's swim, Jill and he would go back to the hotel to make love. It was never after Jill had finished her mango smoothy. Jack liked to describe his love-making as being urgent, it made him feel manly. More often than not, Jill simply felt she was being used, which made her feel lonely.

WELL, FUCK ME, MR DARWIN.

There's obsequiousness in our attachment to the biological, it conveniently explains just about everything from birth to death, and in so doing deprives us of the chance of any deeper understanding of our being. In short, fuck you, Mr Darwin. Might it not be possible that given the gift of consciousness we could rise to some greater urge than the biological/procreative construct? What about

the urge for re-creation, or even the urge for pre-creation? It's the starlight factor, the sound of one hand.

In referring to the biological, we refer firstly to the construct of it, and secondly to what within it might confirm that construct as a reality. *"It's only human nature, so what can I do about it?"* A profound case of self-fulfilment through self-denial: the serpent devouring its own tail. Is there to be no intimate physical contact beyond the common, grunting vulgarities of the biological? "Human nature" is a cop-out. Human nature? Try this and see who comes out on top: *"I am beyond love."*

There can be no revolution until we conclusively dismiss Darwin's primitive, self-protecting theories of evolution. Meanwhile, Lilith takes flight, for she knows no other way.

Jack looks at his watch. It is ten-forty-five, which is five minutes later than ten-forty. He doesn't get the joke. Jill looks at her hands. They're covered in rainbow-coloured bubbles. She feels like a space-angel, but doesn't really know what a space-angel is.

LILITH THE LULLABYE

Jack has been in what he calls a partnership with Jill for ten or so years. Jack wanted a dog, but not children. As a form of unspoken agreement, they had neither. Jack resented this lack of freedom. Why shouldn't he have a dog? Jack bought a car for Jill, a smaller one than his. He said it was a *"perfect lady's car"*. Jill said that she wasn't a perfect lady. Jack said that he was glad and shoved his hands up her blouse. Jill recoiled.

Jill has been in what she calls a relationship with Jack for thirteen years. Jill wanted a child, but not a dog. As a form of unspoken agreement, she had an abortion when she became pregnant. Jill resented having to make this decision. Why shouldn't she have a child? Jack bought her a car as a form of apology, but it was small and she wanted a four-wheel drive like her friends. Jack said that they were really impractical unless you had children or dogs. Jill resented what she saw as the insensitivity of his remark. Jack said *"oh come on, love"*, and stuck his hands up her blouse. Jill recoiled, reached for the kitchen knife and lunged it into his stomach. Jack survived the attack, Jill didn't.

[NOTE] Many years ago I was in a recording studio producing an album of poetry and music. The poems were what could loosely be described as mystical, and the music a soft blend of classical and jazz. The vocalist was Eve Libertine, the front-woman from the anarchist punk band Crass. It was her first public

effort at singing rather than shouting. Her voice was angelic. The album was called "Acts of Love", which should give a further clue. One of the more poignant poems ended with the lines *"In your time, I live. When you awake, I shall awake. Let us live together, we could love each other."* For some reason Eve found the musical setting particularly difficult and had spent a long evening struggling to get it right. At times both of us lost patience with each other, bitterly arguing over fine details which in all probability no one else on earth would have noticed. The atmosphere was anything but loving. Eventually Eve came up with an extraordinarily beautiful take, so I asked her through to the control room to give it a listen. I considered it perfect, but then she said *"I think you should listen through it again."* "But why?" I responded, *"it's in the can."* "Listen to it," she ordered. The engineer ran back the tape and pressed play. *"In your time, I live. When you awake, I shall awake. Let us live together, we could loathe each other."* Point taken.

Jack died from "complications" aged fifty-three. Jill survived him.
She lives in Buckinghamshire with a dog.
R.D. Laing died aged sixty-two.

PART TWO – THE MEANING OF DEATH

"Why is there anything rather than nothing?
Is it only death which gives meaning to life?"
Heidegger

The meaning of death is that in having no time to consider itself, nor even to see its own face, it has no meaning. Death doesn't mind who you are, because to death you are not, which is why it isn't inhabited by the clumsy ghouls of self-consciousness which so pollute its alter-ego, life. Death gets on with itself far away from the conceits of mankind; a glorious domain of silence where the bells have no ringer and the ringer no voice. How, then, did we manage to clamber from its thrall onto the thrusting surfboard of existence?

QUESTION: **how is it Christ died for our sins two thousand years before we committed them?**

ANSWER: **how is it Christ died for our sins two thousand years before we committed them?**

QUESTION: **how is it so often the question is the answer?**

ANSWER: **how is it so often the answer is the question?**

Unless we are each one of us isolated entities, temporally and spatially unique, life is the living proof that there is life after death. Where the hell else do we come from? We *are* the life after death. We are not born "whole", nor as an "expression" of the absolute, for we *are* the absolute, always have been and always will be. It's never been any different: sole and soul, absolute. In that context we are both entirely individual and entirely not so: the one, the all, the everything and the nothing. In short, we are no more alive than we are dead: absolute, and don't let Mr Ego tell you otherwise.

Being mind-based, the spiritual life is as much a denial of the body as it is a denial of the soul: spirituality is a human construct contrived to give word to the wordless soul. If we'd been meant to be angels, we'd have been born with wings. Likewise, if the soul had been meant to speak, it would have been given a mouth. Then flap away, Icarus, and chant your bile, you holy men, I'll have none of it. Spirituality is a corruption, religion a heresy. It's a poor thought that falls for sentimentality. Nietzsche was wrong. God is not dead for he was never alive.

Listen then, you gurus and priests, shamans and prophets,
spirituality is as much
a defilement of soul
as is gross materialism.
That'll be ten shillings and sixpence, in the hat, and don't look for any change.

As much as death is indivisible from the tragic beauty of life, so birth is indivisible from the tragic beauty of death. If we exist at all, we exist as the passion between life and death. There is no innocence, no Garden of Eden, only the wild passion. And here's another thing which is for certain: we have no substance. The ground is only there to fall on in our delusion.

[NOTE] I'm tumbling. I want to be confused no more. I'm tumbling. I toss a bunch of white roses into the mouth of the River Tyne and watch my parents tear themselves apart and submit to the tides. They drift in the Congo, drift in the Zambezi, drift in the Marmara. I fuck a sylph-like young woman up against a white marble column. She's wearing a white lace corset and white lace stockings. Her fanny-hair is black. As history re-describes itself, the church of San Sophia crumbles to dust, the Sphinx devours the meatless bones of childhood and, according to tradition, the unborn throw themselves into the crater of Mount Etna.

THE COLOSSUS OF RHODES STRADDLES THE OCEAN.
Apollo falls to the tempest
and poetry is no more.

As body and mind we are idea separated by idea, a hopeless collusion of falsehood

seduced by our own prejudice, a form of psychic auto-erotica. Gagged by Eve's apple, we joylessly drip our rancid seminal juices into the sodden grave of lost possibilities. Imagining ourselves to be, we become our own moment by moment executioner, yet in being we are no more. *"Oh yes, this is the life,"* and then we fall.

"I love your body, love your mind."
Untrue: I love my own prejudices,
my own construct, my own idea of you.
Mirror that if you like,
but it'll have nothing to do with you.

The mirror cannot see itself nor speak its own mind. Who is this, then, who stares back so vacantly? Who am I? Where are you? Am I you? Are you I? Silence, and then removal.

May the devil ride my soul.
Within the consensual,
death is the only truth.
All else is conjecture.

I observed age, and age looked back, but could not shoulder me away. I watched the seasons come and go, but I remained intact. I might have heard another call, for calamity sings a pretty tune, never so far away from gasp and sigh where old and young cast their fate and then lay themselves down to die. And is it out of humour that we know of death's coming, that Pierrot, pale-faced and cross-eyed, tips the bucket? And although we know the trickery of it, still we thrill, forever waiting, wanting that final spill. In seeing life as ebbing, we encourage the tide, and if Canute could not see through that, how are we otherwise to decide? Oh, the vanities which decide our fate. The painted face knows not its owner, nor callous meaning a smile, yet still we wait.

The primal determines point of view,
yet it is not the primal which sees.
The astral knows no wit.

Fear is the thrall, the kidnapping of soul, and what the greatest fear if it is not death? Then already the soul is stolen and already we are dead. So what the fear but an idea of life? Sing me the sad tune that I may know the thunder, or perhaps the scythe to open meadow and to mow down the poppies. I do believe that out there there's a kingdom laid in blood.

**That you were gone to savannah
without a word.
Do you not know that in the beginning
was the word?
Then let us seek an ending.**

Each moment we die, hysterical in our self-romance. Each moment we rise again, a constant journey between being and non-being, yet it is not with non-being that we are most familiar. Then our being is at best half-being, a half life, and how clumsily we carry it, hobbling down sordid sidewalks littered with the detritus of false desire. How can we exist by that alone?

**Knowing that remission is the glue twixt
life and death, our only salvation,
I sing a song of saviour,
but I am not saved myself.**

**Truth is born
in the lap of lies.**

Death is the "only" by another name. Then is not that other name also mine?

AM I NOT ALREADY DEAD?

PART THREE - THE MEANING OF IMMORTALITY

*"The crowd by its very concept is the untruth by reason of the fact
that it renders the individual irresponsible."*
Kierkegaard

Between being and non-being exists the state of immortality. The King shall wear his crown and the Christ carry his crucifix, but I am transient, impermanent. In between the cross and its body, the brow and its crown, neither bloody nor tearful, I lay me down to rest awhile.

In the great ocean of soul there is no separateness, no illness, no disease, no suffering, no death, which is also to say there is no life. Nonetheless, consciousness allows for ideas of detachment, a sense of removal and, however unprovable, a sense of life. Within that removal we are able to form constructs which prevail against soul, against the absolute. In that sense, human existence is an act of denial, a refusal to engage in the dynamics of life and death, no more than a temporary enclosure.

"Hell is other people," said Sartre,
**conveniently forgetting that
he was one of them.**

Given its longevity, the domain of consciousness is extraordinarily small. Our families are nuclear, our friendships few, our emotional and intellectual dependency on this paucity enormous. Acting as an umbrella to our myopic, blinkered existence, Hollywood and the media flood our consciousness with a hypnotic fantasy which is nothing short of Oz-like in its proportions. Drowning in seas of trivia, from caravan deaths to 9/11, to whom or what do we call for salvation or even absolution? Within this savage utopia, Murdoch has become the wonderful wizard, the terrible unmentionable übermensch. There are many more.

"Forgive me, father, for I cannot feel the rain."

Then what is this laundered parkland through which we wander so aimlessly? Or is it, as I have often observed before, a macrocosmic death camp? "Arbeit macht frei." And so we wilfully throw ourselves into the oven mouth, half-baked and half-cocked. Burn, sisters, burn. Burn, brothers, burn.

THIS IS CHRIST'S REALITY ASYLUM:
had I been there to suck
CHRIST'S COCK
in the agony of his crucifixion, might he have smiled just once and known joy?

Beyond our own conceits and the enclosures of definition, we can and do exist untouched by the overwhelming violence of the consensual world. Conclusive proof of this can be found in that against impossible odds we are able to sleep and, furthermore, wake up again. In sleep we know not who we are, and nor do we in that moment of awakening before the consensual world floods again into our consciousness. It is during those times that we roam free in a limitless cosmos, beyond the primal, as stardust again. That is our right, our heritage, yet how studiously we avoid that call to what most perceive as non-being, yet is in fact the only truth of being: shining, limitless, eternal, immortal. The state of death.

So what is our identity but a malicious joke, an act of unbridled viciousness against the unconditional divinity of existence? Do we then choose to exist in name alone, exiled from life, or as the cutting blade which consensually is known as death, but which I know to be the soft brush of eternity's wings?

Either my love is all, or it is nothing.

As self-defined, self-enclosed identities we imagine ourselves to be detached from the force of life and removed from its fate. Why else the palaces and castles? Why else the key and lock? Why else the cosmetic mask and the sham of emotion? It is enclosure which holds us back from the wilds, enclosure which feeds us the falsification of desire. We play the hunter, but we dare not kill. We play the lover, but we dare not love. Happy enough to be the bobbing boat in the restless storms of the consensual, we dare not dive to those oceanic depths for fear we may be suffocated by the weight.

Happier to be the meniscus than the flow. Happier to live a living death rather than to embrace the timeless silence of immortality.

Transfixed by fear, we concentrate our energies on that which most makes us fearful, and in so doing prescribe a temporal fate which in reality is no more than a self-fulfilling construct. Meanwhile, shoals of reptilian professionals, academics, doctors, lawyers and bastard bankers wearing the black suit of the devil and noosed tie of the executioner, hunt out prey in the river of tears flooded by our lonely fears. These are the maggots, the parasites; the very devils who believe that they can suck dry the soul and gnaw away the absolute. But it is we who permit them that folly.

If doubt there be, doubt is thee, hung upon thy cross.

By concentrating our energies on the negative, be it physical or mental, we give weight to that which depends on that weight for its existence. Cancer and AIDS are prime examples of negative constructs dependant for their existence upon negative projections. Enter the devils, the prognosis, the death sentence.

[NOTE] In a "field test" carried out in a Zimbabwean hospital, of twenty patients showing the same symptoms, ten were admitted as having AIDS, while the other ten were sent home and told to eat more. While the ten admitted patients were all dead within a month, the ten sent home survive to this day.

The body wants to survive. It has no option. But the mind, lazy and irresponsible, prefers to engage in the easy and the obvious, to marry into the banal, to sacrifice the body in the temple of consensual trash. How else the tiresome soap-operas, the repetitive schmaltz of the pop world, the turgid trash of the tabloids? This, then, is our psychic diet: the physical and psychological gadgets and geegaws which determine that we rise not from the sickbed of half-being, but prefer rather to drift helpless into old age, sickness and death.

AND THUS SPAKE ZARATHUSTRA, GOD BLESS HIS SOUL.

And if our mortality taunts us, it does so to deny us the greater power of immortality, yet we are singular voice to both: the reign of silence. We exist as verb, then how are we become noun? Why cast the net into charted seas to draw silvered fish to parched sands? Why turn the cogs of convention to prove a worth already established by our being? Why stumble to chattering moraine seeking out the dog-ends of existence?

Narcissus bore himself
    that no other could bear him.
The reflection was changeling:
    preoccupation and obsession.
But now the tarn is dried up
    and there is no more than crust.

But we are not flotsam.
We are absolution,
for we are absolute.
We are grace,
for we exist before ourselves.
All else is contrivance.

The path we know is illusion, for knowledge knows only itself. There is nowhere to go. The mighty cat stretches out upon the rock awaiting the strike. It knows not what or where, yet it is built for all these things. Well then, when it leaps, tangle with its claws that you might not doubt its force. The mighty cat is forever feral, determined only that it shall not be determined. Stolid conformity sees little but the space it leaves behind, but we know the taste of blood, or else deny ourselves the gift of it.

So smug we are in deliberation, slicing life apart with such considered precision, but it is fear which is the thrall, the adhesion. Fear, the kidnapper of soul, the derision, and what again the greatest fear? But if Grim Reaper there be, then he must be you, must be I, must be we: the preparation.

THOU SHALT
NOT

But fear not,
    for death is the great comforter,
        the great leveller.
We are impotent against that calling,
    and if we are blind to that,
        then that will be our falling.

In the joyous carnival of immortality there is no quest, but in the slaughterhouse of false connection everything is set in terms of opposition, for it is there that we define ourselves *through* opposition.

But there is no debate. In our containment of self we signify nothing. Before we were named, we were the celebration, the light before the moment, the day before The Creation.

The goat cannot be proved by the sheep.

That thou shalt, so thou wilt, for thou art.
There can be no denial of that.
We are nobody's child but our own.

THOU ART.

We cannot know ourselves
if in any way we hide from each other.

THEN
HIDE
NOT

HIDE NOT

If you think you've got the answer, you didn't hear the question.

Text Penny Rimbaud · *Portrait* Jean-Paul Berthoin · *Typesetting* Christian Brett at Bracketpress

University?
Don't Bother

IF YOU WANT TO GET AHEAD, THEN AVOID THE UNIVERSITY, SAYS LECTURER L.A. ROWLAND. **ILLUSTRATIONS BY** JOANNA WALSH

I say with neither pride nor prejudice that I am the only person from my family to have been through university. Coming from a long line of soldiers, carpenters, and stonemasons, it was never expected that I would; but an opportunity to take A-levels at night school during my twenties meant that, as a mature student, I entered the academy on a journey that led to my current position lecturing in psychology at a highly prestigious university. So for those of you reading this who are unsure about what to do with your future, as all spirited young people should be, and are considering higher education as an option, then let me give you some free and very useful advice: don't bother.

Ten years after I set out to seek knowledge, I've realised that there's nothing august about universities, no higher truth they're working towards. Under nobler command they could have been places of conceptual magnanimity and beauty, but left exposed to the ravages of the base end of human nature, they have matured into something stooping and ugly. With the glittering new campuses, the influx of students and the high-profile academics, one is enticed to believe otherwise. The same forces are at work when a child sees McDonalds. After decades of under funding, many UK institutions suffer financial crisis, but this will change as they become increasingly geared to making money. Consequently, as places of true learning, wisdom, and originality they are withering rapidly. To be a part of this, one must spend a small fortune on an education that trains you be like everyone else.

The lure of university for many is that it offers promise and hope for the future, with particular respect to money and career. It is foolish to believe that a greater amount of education is integral to obtaining these, as the majority of musicians, actors, businessmen and entrepreneurs will attest, but for those who are less talented or less ambitious, it may well be that average earnings over one's lifetime are higher with letters after your name. Or certainly it has been so. It is highly contestable whether this is likely to be the case from hereon in: it will only be apparent in thirty or forty years whether, after the enormous expansion of student numbers that we are witnessing, this assertion is borne out. But it is telling that already there are reports in the media about graduates re-training to be plumbers, electricians, and carpenters. Often, better job prospects, more job satisfaction, and higher earnings motivate them to look further afield than human resources and IT.

As a psychologist, I suggest that those who are successful in the corporate world, or any capitalist venture, are so because of their personality and their acquired system of values, rather than thanks to a university education. A very good school friend of mine went straight to work at the local bank without even pausing to do A-levels. He now earns more than four times the salary of both myself and a few other close friends who all opted for the learned route. Whilst discussing this article with my twenty-one-year-old cousin, I discovered that she is in charge of eighteen people at the Barclays call centre where she is a team leader. Five of her team have been to university, whereas she left school after obtaining a fairly ordinary set of A-levels. Furthermore, one of her friends has just gone to Manchester to study music management. She is hell bent on becoming a talent scout. If I were a record boss, I wouldn't take on anyone who lacked such ingenuity that they felt that education was necessary for spotting the next great band.

Idealists may object that the principal reason for entering higher education is to learn and think. This was my own view when I began, but I now see that it is impossible to create an institution where the attitudes of those running it are not imbibed by the lower ranks. Try organising an army where the generals are all pacifists. Modern universities are not anything to do with real learning, and it's worth questioning whether they ever really were. The University of Bologna, one of Europe's oldest and most distinguished, began as a law school, not a haven for men of passion and learning. It saddens me that all the polytechnics were transposed into universities, and now all the universities are reverting to something like a polytechnic. The new credo, unimaginatively supported by the unctuous Charles Clarke, is that universities and their products must exist for the benefit of the economy. The weeds of the applied disciplines are impoverishing the fertile topsoil that flowers the arts and philosophy.

This profiteering mentality is changing the nature of the learning experience. As Oxford is poised to introduce Harvard-style fees, insiders believe its small group tutorial system, which is elemental to its appeal and success, is set to be abolished. It is simply too expensive to maintain. Ironically, the system is threatened by the large numbers of students initially brought in to boost the wealth of the university through expansion. As with the bleak environmental outlook, the myopia of the capitalist view blurs the horizon, and may well be our undoing.

The availability of Masters degrees has ramified in recent years, thus exploiting an anxious market of young people concerned with their image on paper in our prosaic

CV-obsessed culture. The institutions love these courses because they are easy to set up, require little teaching time and have low administrative costs, yet they cost the students an arm and a leg, especially if they hail from overseas, which unsurprisingly many do. But they have little to do with learning. You should try discussing continental philosophy amongst 17 intellectual aspirants in an hour's seminar and see if you come out anything other than depressingly baffled and thoroughly jarred-off.

WHAT WE'RE LEFT WITH IS THE NOTION OF UNIVERSITY AS A SERVICE, NOT AS A CREATIVE ENTERPRISE

These changes are indicative of a wider cultural problem, where nothing is seen to have any intrinsic worth unless it can be measured or quantified or graded in some way. Hence we have petty university league tables, restrictive research targets to meet, and meaningless teaching scores. The twentieth century's greatest philosopher, Ludwig Wittgenstein, was renowned for his so-called lectures where he did nothing more than sit and discuss an idea with his students, often something that he had just been thinking about that very morning. The class would sit in silence for minutes at a time whilst Wittgenstein stared into space and thought through an argument. Of course, those privileged enough to have been taught by him knew that they were learning by experiencing true creative thought in action. Nowadays he wouldn't be allowed near a lecture theatre. Instead they send in someone who can tell you everything they've read about Wittgenstein but didn't really understand.

What we're left with is the notion of education as a service, not as a creative enterprise. The problem with this view is that true knowledge cannot be delivered; it must be sought. Worryingly, most students make it through university without reading a single academic book all the way through. In order to get good grades it is more expedient to mix and match from many sources, cutting and pasting information tailored to passing exams. Reading a whole classic book will waste too much time and does not guarantee exam success. I cannot tell you how many people in psychology can quote the great William James without ever having seen, let alone read, his classic *The Principles of Psychology*. Yet many pundits regard this the single greatest work in psychology. One reviewer asserts that James's masterpiece "ought to be read from beginning to end at least once by every person professing to be educated." In this competitive environment there's no time for sitting under a tree whiling the time away beguiled by a nineteenth century masterpiece.

In fact, the introduction of signed compulsory attendance agreements will make idling at university the preserve of the diehard rebel. Students who do not stick to the timetable, as required in schools, will, after a warning, be expelled. Such measures are unspeakable, but they are upon us. They will benefit those who shouldn't really be at university in the first place: those who need to hold the firm hand of continuous assessment. Many of the truly great original thinkers could not have succeeded in such a system. Einstein and John Nash revolutionised physics and economics respectively precisely because they were allowed the space and time to dream.

There is the possibility that university is still the place where you will meet the most cultured and interesting people, and that you may in turn emerge with these qualities. Truly, this is down to the individual and his or her childhood and has nothing to do with higher education. Many characters of the utmost renown and refinement found no need for the cap and gown. William Shakespeare is but one excellent example. A stifling and clichéd environment may quash such native force, and therefore I recommend that those who wish to cultivate a more unique intelligence steer clear of the hallowed halls. My brother, despite enviable ability, has refused to go to university and has endured hardship and rejection as a substitute. At thirty-one years of age, things are really starting to come together for him now as a writer and documentary maker, and I'm quite sure that his bespangled personality and unconventional cognitions have flourished directly because he chose the warrior's path.

Everyone who I have asked has said that they wouldn't change the experience for anything, but a moment's reflection has led me to think that university is no better than any other challenging and exploratory venture. I was once a soldier, and I found that to be more rewarding, more challenging, more fun, and more exciting than the three years spent doing a degree. Certainly my soldier mates were wittier and more life-affirming lads than any of the goons I met as an undergraduate.

I don't imagine that universities were always thus. I like to daydream about the old times when scholars and students were left alone to get on with it themselves. No one questioned their importance to society, and consequently, unhindered by cloying bureaucracy and poncey governments, they were places of vigour, radicalism and creativity. Such sensibilities were out of step with the inexorable rise of twentieth century capitalism, and slowly but surely our great learning institutions succumbed. What we see now is that entering university is a leap onto the escalator that takes you down to the basement of capitalism. There are no windows down there: it is dark. Only by a supreme effort of the will can you find your own way out of this vast and impersonal space. People are on hand to promise a way out, but in return you will have to work very hard at learning to say the same things as all those who went before you. You will need to pay lots of money for this privilege, and there are many people willing to lend. Finally, a graduate fast-track scheme offers a lift up to ground level, but in reality you're just shoved through the emergency exit amongst the rubbish bins to make way for the new arrivals. Unless you run immediately, the rest of your life will be spent there.

There is no room for mavericks in this system. Everyone must be seen to be doing his or her bit, and everyone must do it willingly. I know of one charismatic lecturer who was being squashed out by the powers that be because she wasn't producing *enough* top quality research, although the work she did was of a high standard. She also refused to stop smoking out of her office window, and often defied convention with her bizarre outfits. As a teacher she was one of the best I have known.

This stultifying environment repels the people who would give it colour. Wittgenstein's education in philosophy began when he turned up out of the blue at Bertrand Russell's door in Cambridge one morning. He didn't enrol on a philosophy degree until much later. Nowadays this is utterly inconceivable. To modern academics students are seen as a nuisance and not as people from whom they too can learn. With so many poor students, I have some sympathy with this view. Yet in this prevailing hierarchical atmosphere, opportunities to mix socially with lecturers and professors are virtually nil, which ultimately fosters a dull and uninspiring climate. In the competitive market of academic capital no one can afford to be eccentric and carefree. Instead they are career driven and harassed. One of my old professors at UCL could regularly be seen ambling round the squares of Bloomsbury stopping and admiring the flowers whilst all the others rushed past him on the way to meetings. University is no longer aegis for the contemplative loafer.

Modern-day academics work tirelessly at research that bolsters their reputation and raises the profile of their department. The number of articles published each week in any discipline is dizzying, and I believe that most of it is unnecessary. For true knowledge seekers, the confusion created by this rapid proliferation of useless information is of course disheartening. The Socratic Method recognised that confusion is good because it is directed towards wisdom, but this is only true if one admits to the confusion. Today's scholars aim to eliminate confusion by becoming evermore specialised: no one can be a polymath these days; it's a lifetime's work keeping abreast of one's own very narrow specialism. As academic trades go, there are no masters and no jacks. I am fascinated by my subject, but I do not want to specialise, and I do not want to compete as an internationally renowned researcher. I simply want time to teach those who really want to be taught, and I want time to release my imagination. Recently I took a heavy drop in pay to allow me to do just that. If I am to write something genuinely worthwhile in psychology, it will not be under the auspices of the academy. I will need to strike out alone, far away from the towers of the great unread to the green hills of the free, and there I shall begin to untangle what I have learned.

I implore our young people, in particular those with courage and ability, to find their own way to knowledge, if that is what they seek. If you hanker for adventure, be fearless and fanciful. Care not for the conventions of the corporate workplace, and muster the confidence and vigour to create work for yourself, playing to your talents, not to titles bestowed by an institution that does not know you. As William James was aware in 1903, "...no man of science or letters will be accounted respectable unless some kind of badge or diploma is stamped upon him, and in which bare personality will be a mark of outcast estate. It seems to me high time to rouse ourselves to consciousness, and to cast a critical eye upon this decidedly grotesque tendency."

Anyone for whom it is not too late should save their parents' money, avoid debt, and use the time to educate themselves in their own fashion. Start with *The Principles of Psychology*, then you shall feel justifiably proud. 🔊

MEMORANDA

The Road
to Evian

IN 2003, PHOTOGRAPHER IMMO KLINK
DOCUMENTED A BLOCKADE PROTEST AT
THE G8 SUMMIT AT EVIAN

DNA DL90 BY ABIGAIL FALLIS, A 35FT DOUBLE HELIX OF SHOPPING TROLLEYS, NOW SHOWING AT THE
CASS FOUNDATION, GOODWOOD, EAST SUSSEX

Shop Local

TONY WHITE **WRITES IN
PRAISE OF THE PROPER SHOP
AND ATTACKS SUPERMARKET
BABYLON. YEA!**

DARLING.
EVERYONE OR NO ONE.
THE ENTIRE HUMAN RACE.
MY FAMILY.

Come captains and job seekers and schoolmasters and dockers and dinnerladies and hoodies and artificers and magistrates and sign-holders and wardens and restaurateurs and attendants and assistants and chuggers and boy-racers and teachers and editors and mechanics and oily rags and engineers and scientists and nurses and bar-staff and secretaries and production assistants and petitioners and respondents and asylum seekers and locksmiths and claimants and hackers and milkmen and key grips and best boys and sparks and chippies and single mothers and electricians and builders and reps and philanthropists and farmers and cooks and brokers and bureaucrats and solicitors and idlers and postmen and diggers and dancers and DJs and web designers and photographers and and drivers and all you regiments of humanity. Come customers. Gather round and let us make of these beautiful shops an Oasis of friendly service, quality products and sustainable commerce for the benefit of all!

Bring the Ranters and noncomformists–bring Abiezer Coppe[1] a.k.a. Mr Hiam, latterly of Barnes and buried in Barnes churchyard August 23 1672, bring Isaac Pennington the Younger[2], bring Thomas Carlyle[3]–bring pamphleteers and bill-posters, bring the Friends of the Earth briefing on *How to… Oppose a Supermarket Planning Application* and fold them in one against the other. Bring pink and yellow fluorescent card and black marker pens. Stick notices up behind your tills and petitions on your counters.

DO NOT ASK FOR CREDIT AS A SMACK IN THE MOUTH OFTEN OFFENDS[4]

The proposals came upon me like a great thunderclap and upon the second thunderclap I saw a great body of light, like the light of the sun, and where, rapt up in silence, at length I heard with my outward ear (to my apprehension) that a second 30,000 sq ft net Class A1 convenience footstore with 350 parking spaces, 17 disabled parking spaces and 12 parent and child spaces would be built. Whereupon with exceeding trembling and unspeakable fear in the spirit, I beheld the landscaping and boundary treatments and the improved vehicle and pedestrian access. *Amen.* But there was already nearby a modern main (bulk) food store and numerous smaller shops from Barn Elms to the river designed to meet the existing needs of my dearest friends, so I was rammed and sunk into nothing, and into the bowels of its surrounding catchment area.

And all this terror and amazement did provide a broad range of convenience products accounting for the transcendent unspeakable glory that comprises a retail sales area. The store will also provide, for comparison, darkness (you must take it in these terms) and 9,500 sq ft for sundry non-food items which are typically sold in such stores: seasonal products, clothes, pet foods, videos/CDs, a selection of heavily discounted books, newspapers, magazines, sweets and cigarettes, and small items of homeware that the typical main food-shopping trip may also include some breath and life and impulse buys. Whereupon I saw various streams of

....

[1] Abiezer Coppe, A Fiery Flying Roll, 1650 • [2] Isaac Pennington the Younger, Babylon the Great Described, 1659 • [3] Thomas Carlyle, Latter Day Pamphlets, 1850

light and great banners and free plastic carrier bags providing the quality of service and high standards demanded of a food retailer. The store will also provide a major universality, a distinction, a diversity and a general availability of main food shopping opportunities the majority of which are available for the main bulk food shopping of same dear friends, but at their own expense, for cheapness comes at a price.

It was exceeding terrible. My strength and my forces were utterly routed. I felt as if my house had been demolished, that my old name was rotted, perished; that my mum and dad had chucked me out and I was utterly plagued, consumed and damned.

NO MORE THAN TWO SCHOOL CHILDREN AT ONE TIME

If I ruled the world, certainly it wouldn't be the supermarkets that I would first of all concentrate my attention upon! Supermarkets? I should be apt to make rather brief work with them; to them I would apply the broom and try to sweep them with some rapidity into the dust bin. But this new supermarket is Babylon. And Babylon is the spiritual fabric of iniquity.

1. It is a shop. This is a proper parable, to discover the mystery of iniquity and how it can be consistent with the need to maintain and enhance the function of existing town centres.

2. Thus it is that there are a great many aisles and shelves and parking spaces in this shop and they have their own laws and government pertaining to them yet should not adversely affect the vitality and viability of an existing shopping centre.

3. Their several services, places, offices and employments must be consistent with the need for urban regeneration, particularly the revitalisation of town and city centres.

4. It is a spiritual or mystical shop, it is not just an outward building of earthly materials but an inward building of inward materials, yet must be readily accessible by public transport, cyclists and pedestrians.

5. It is a great shop; an overspreading shop, and is sited so as to reduce the need to travel by car.

6. It is a shop of hidden iniquity yet it must be well related to, but not adversely affect residential areas.

....

[4] With thanks to Steve Beard

CUSTOMERS MUST CHECK LOTTERY NUMBERS ARE CORRECT BEFORE LEAVING THE SHOP, THANKYOU.

It hid, keeping its life under a covering of uniform modern design, as forecast in the Retail Study. Convenience was hid under zeal, under devotion, under brand, and included an allowance for tourist spending. What lies hid within under these, there is Babylon, there is £26.5 million of investment in 2006 and a further £2.36 million in 2007. While the survey findings also have many changes and turnings, and are illustrated with numerous figures, tables and artists impressions, there is however the potential for this or that (being the sense or meaning of such development) to claw-back a leakage from the catchment area. They estimate to retain approximately one-third (35%) of convenience and approximately two-thirds (65%) of burning and utter desolation.

SIM CARDS ALL NETWORKS £6.99

Other material considerations concerning which much more might be said were that the proposed store will deliver a great and mighty city. Oh the power of widely accessible locations! Thereby lying about the wonders that are there shown: direct benefits! Wages! Life! To persuade men and women that the Chief Executive thereof is into the local economy with benefits to those suppliers and hope &c. that some qualitative improvements are provided within the area, providing of course that the Elect, by the opening of the eternal eye, can reduce both the number and length of car-journeys without losing the resulting consumer sustainability benefits.

The proposed store will also deliver major regeneration. And regenerate a site in close proximity to the town centre in all the shapes and forms of it, to every street and every house, every chamber, every likeness, every duty and every promise. Moreover, there is painted the provision of modern new utilities and recreational facilities, namely here is building up and throwing down, and here are crèches, cafes, pharmacists, a postal micro-concession and public swimming pools. Then away! And down go a series of largely unused light-industrial units, and down go hedges and trees, and on with her building and up with her plan!

JAMES THE GREATER, WITH HOT DOG, FROM THE FAST SUPPER BY ABIGAIL FALLIS, PAPIER MACHÉ AND NEWSPAPER, 2006.

CUSTOMER WISHING TO USE DEBIT/CREDIT CARD FOR TABACO, ALCOHOL, LOTTERY, INTERNATIONAL PHONE CARD, MOBILE TOP-UP WILL BE CHARGE £1.50

Oh London, London. Oh Anytown. My bowels are rolled together in me for out-of-town and brownfield supermarkets and now I only tell you it was not in vain that this form has expanded at a massive rate. But to proclaim that campaigners are not giving up, in fact all over the country with their hands fiercely stretched out, building alliances with other local groups and with a mighty voice they are speaking out to decision makers in their areas. It *is* possible to oppose their greatest ranks!

Away, you, begone swiftly, supermarkets; in the name of God and his poor struggling servants, shop keepers and sole traders, sore put to it to live in these bad days. See them with crossed tobacco-pipes and crossed red-herrings in their windows to keep Babylon at bay and not enlist with them. Others have diverse notices, signs and stickers in their windows: for Paypoint, that people might pay their bills monthly or refill their pre-payment meters, for "bus passes and travel cards sold here", for Oyster, for the *Evening Standard* "Save our small shops" campaign, for Coca Cola, for Walls, for rooms to let, for Old Skool night at Hammersmith Palais, for the National Lottery, for deliveries, for freshly baked croissants ("Real French, Real Fresh"), for top-ups, for telephone cards, for "ATM Inside".

POLISH SPECIALITIES: TU KUPISZ POLSKI-CHLEB!

And what? These newsagents and greasy-spoons and record shops and book shops and greengrocers and cheese shops and toy-shops and junkshops and fishmongers and butchers and internet cafés and chemists and drapers and gift shops and outfitters and delicatessens and pound shops and off-licences and market stalls and cobblers and key-cutters and grocers and cafés and bakers and hardware stores and jewellers and family businesses (est. 1872!) and antique shops and workshops &c to close? No, by God! I have quite other work for that class of artists!

IF THE LIGHTS ARE ON
WE ARE STILL OPEN[5]

Then raise a glass for The Barnes Fish Shop Ltd ("Got any squid?")! Raise a glass for J. Seal the butcher! Raise a glass for Natsons, newsagents of the year! Raise a glass for Villa Fern and The Hardware Store! Raise a glass for Gusto and Relish on White Hart Lane (and oppose the revised supermarket proposal for the former Jaguar Showroom—sign the petition in Pat's Food Store)! Raise a glass for Valentina's Italian Food and Wine in East Sheen! Raise a glass for V&G Barbers on Church Road! Raise a glass for Haircut on Camden High Street! Raise a glass for the Quality Food Store on Cannon Street Road! Raise a glass (no corkage charged!) for New Tayyabs on Fieldgate Street! Raise a glass for independent bookshops everywhere! Cheers, friends! See you on Saturday and all Saturdays to come.

This story was written for Bob and Roberta Smith's *Shop Local* project for the Peer Trust and first appeared in a slightly different form in the *Shop Local* pamphlet.

FURTHER READING

Corporatewatch: www.corporatewatch.org.uk
The New Economics Foundation (resources including the 'Tools for Local Economic Renewal' project): www.neweconomics.org
The Council for the Protection of Rural England: www.planninghelp.org.uk
The Planning Portal: www.planningportal.gov.uk
Planning Aid: www.planningaid.org.uk
Download the Friends of the Earth Briefing, *How to… Oppose a Supermarket Planning Application* at: www.foe.co.uk/resource/briefings/campaigning_against_super-markets.pdf
The Tescopoly Alliance: www.tescopoly.org
Asda Watch: www.asdawatch.org

[5] The motto of The Barnes Fish Shop Ltd.

From the Pen of
Jock Scot

THIS ISSUE JOCK HAS A GOOD FUCKIN' MOAN

The word "protest" immediately has me thinking of the protest movement of the sixties, when mainly young students demonstrated outside public buildings or occupied campuses, protesting about racial inequality and later, the war in Vietnam.

I was young at the time, born in 1952, but those scenes on the family TV screen and in newspapers left a marked impression. By the mid-sixties I was a member of the Young Communist League, Musselburgh Branch. The local cinema, outside the jurisdiction of Edinburgh Corporation, showed films which had been refused a certificate uptown. Movies like "Fanny Hill" brought the "dirty mac" brigade to town and caused traffic jams and reactionary comment in the local press. This curious loophole and its real intrusion into my life led directly to my first participation in a demonstration. A group of us Young Commies took it upon ourselves to protest outside the local Playhouse cinema over the screening, not of some weak, soft-porn offering, but of

the Vietnam goes to Hollywood war film "The Green Berets" wherein John Wayne flew the flag and whupped the Gooks. Musselburgh Y.C.L. were supporters of Muhammed Ali's stance on that particular conflict. We berated the "Duke's" film fans in squeaky, adolescent voices, before heading off down the local caff for a bottle of Coca-Cola and a Mars bar, [served by a gorgeous waitress who later married Barry Gibb of the Bee Gees] Obviously, she was out of my league and age-group, so I made do with chatting up the more attractive YCL girls while Eric Burdon sang "Sky Pilot", his anti-war-in-Vietnam rock song on the juke-box.

So already, a heady mix of Protest, skirt-chasing and Rock 'n' Roll was entwining and overgrowing the virgin, verdant pastures of my tiny but ready to expand mind. The drugs came later.

Whilst never having committed a revolutionary act in my life, I've never pulled the trigger of a gun that really did go "Bang!" not even to bring down an overweight gamebird, there are other ways to protest at whatever it is that irks or incenses you, be it the introduction of the unjust and hated Poll Tax on a trial run a year early in Scotland, or the British National Party standing in a local election. My favourite protesters, uniquely British in their expression and protest, are Class War.

I recently met up with their founder, Ian Bone, at the launch of his autobiography, *Bash The Rich: True Life Confessions of an Anarchist in the UK*, and, while this piece is neither a puff for this fine history of their contribution to political protest nor an admission of complete approval of their hilarious antics over the years, the book is a fuckin' hilarious read. My politics vere between those espoused by Comrade Bone and the other towering figure in alternative British politics, the late and greatly missed, Screamin' Lord Sutch. I remember meeting up with David Sutch one pre-election night and asked him what he was doing in Gaz's Rockin' Blues, London's finest nightclub these past thirty years, surely he should be at home penning his election address or canvassing round the doors of his constituency? Fast as shit off a shovel came his succinct reply: "These are my people, and I have come among them on election eve to beg their votes and support." The fact that he was standing for election in Finchley, opposing Margaret Thatcher and Gaz's club was in Soho was neither here nor there to a true revolutionary like the Screamin' Lord.

Pity he lost his deposit again that year.

But once again I digress, to get back to Class War and Bash the Rich. I loved the almost non-violent tenet of their slogan "Bash the Rich." [Even though the most striking cover of their propaganda organ, the Xeroxed mag *Class War* showed a graphic of Maggie with a butcher's cleaver, dripping blood, firmly esconced in her bonce on the cover!] It introduced a humorous element painfully absent from all other political propaganda. I also loved the way that nearly all proceeds from the sale of said publication seemed to find their way into the till of whatever hostelry the Class War cadres were drinking in that day. In those days, before the repeal of the licensing laws, [as a result of Shane MacGowan's howling protest song "Repeal the Licensing Laws"] the revolution could always wait 'til after closing time.

Social commentators and arch-Conservatives will always say that rock'n'roll and the politically-slanted, popular protest song never change a thing, well they would, wouldn't they? They are missing the point. Protest songs provide the soundtrack, if not to revolution, at the very least to social change.

Of course a few turkeys have been released along the way, and not just by the Animal Liberation Front each run-up to Christmas time. Although Nelson Mandela was not eventually released from his wrongful imprisonment JUST because The Specials A.K.A. had a Number one hit with "Free Nelson Mandela." BUT, the songs' success definitely embarrassed the fuck out of the bastards who locked him up, every time it was played, and gave succour and encouragement to all those folk who worked towards securing his eventual release.

Given half a chance, I'll protest about anything that gets my goat, but despite my undoubted talents as a wordsmith I'd rather leave the floor to those whose talents are better suited to writing protest songs, like Joe Strummer.

Things which have got on my tits this century include, off the top o' my head:

The gradual disappearance of Routemaster's, London's reliable, iconic, red bus. Especially as Ken Livingstone had said previously that the Routemaster would not be scrapped;

I object most strongly to being served my pint in a plastic glass;

Unreasonable bureauocracy, implemented by blockheads (usually at gigs) e.g. the no-smoking ban. Fine by me. I'm a former heavy smoker, 40 Piccadilly a day, but gave up last January 7. On a recent visit to Glasgow with my chums, Babyshambles, I was loitering intently around the foyer and felt like having a quick fag (although I have "given up" I don't kill myself over it. If I feel like having a smoke, I have one.) So I said to the doorman, "Is it OK to nip outside and have a quick fag in the street, then come back in?" "No way pal. If you go outside after 9pm you are considered to have left the venue for good." Eh!? "But I've got an Access All Areas pass, and a pass for the Aftershow party. I'm just goin' the other side of that glass door for a roll-up in the wind and rain, obeying the no smoking rule. I'll be five minutes and you'll be able to see me the whole time, then I'll come back in.." "Dinnae get funny wi' me pal. Ony mair o' yer nonsense and I'll huv yee oot." "Power." However miniscule it's brief, should never be given to those without the intelligence to implement and interpret its use.

Uneven paving stones;

Fixed, plastic seats in caffs;

The postman leaving a "we called while you were out" card asking you to collect your parcel from the nearest post office, without first knocking at the door to see if you are in;

Gastropubs. What's happened to all the decent boozers?

Bosnian-Hedges cigarettes;

Unavailability of Irn Bru in a glass bottle outside Scotland;

The price of fireworks.

I could go on moaning but I try to remain an optimist, plus this copy is long overdue. See you in the new year. Cue a long list of classic protest songs of which dear departed Joe was the author. My personal favourite being "Armagideon Time" with the great line "It's not Christmas Time. It's Armagideon Time!" Beautiful! "Know Your Rights!" is another, apart from the odd weak line e.g. "You have the right to food money." Which has always made me cringe.

It's the overall rightness and strength of the lyric and the commitment of Joe's vocal which makes it one of the great protest songs. And Joe was no armchair, champagne socialist. Sure he made a few quid from his talents as a songwriter and performer, but nothin' like what he could've trousered. I recall being on the road with Joe's post-Clash band, Latino Rockabilly War. Doing a benefit tour for, as it happens, Class War. At the Edinburgh gig, the punters had been overcharged something like 25p a ticket and he insisted the money was given back to the public as they left!

Daft, mad, nigh impossible to achieve but the measure of the man. But once again I digress. Or do I? Maybe that little anecdote was a small protest at the way the truth is twisted after the event and those who can no longer defend themselves have their reputation slurred and defaced.

STORIES

The Layabouts

FROM THE NOVEL BY ALBERT COSSERY.
ILLUSTRATIONS BY MIREILLE FAUCHON
TRANSLATED BY LULU NORMAN **AND** ROS SCHWARTZ

IV. It was the sacrosanct hour of siesta; the house was silent, as if buried in the very heart of silence. Sometimes, an imperceptible, muffled sound of washing-up floated in the immobile atmosphere, like a cry drowned through the fog of sleep. Stretched out on his bed, Rafik was not sleeping. His eyes wide open in the half-light, he was taking scrupulous care to stay awake, wearing himself out in an unequal battle against torpor. He was waiting for Haga Zohra, the go-between, whose scheming threatened to throw the whole household into irredeemable chaos. He'd decided that his father's marriage would not take place, even if, to that end, he had to stay awake for several days. It was a bold act, verging on madness, and Rafik was afraid of succumbing to fatigue, of not being equal to his mission. Beads of sweat formed on his forehead; as he tried his utmost to combat the insidious drowsiness taking hold of his limbs, a heavy, slow languor flowed in his veins. The suffering was already beginning. He stiffened, raised himself up onto his elbows and breathed heavily. He heard his own breath and was startled; he'd nearly woken Galal who was asleep in the next bed, his face turned to the wall, completely buried beneath his eiderdown. No breathing ruffled the implacable rigour of his death-like sleep. Rafik wondered at this prodigious obliteration, untroubled by any anxiety. It was an almost comatose state, a lethargy of conscience. For Galal, there'd been no choice; his sleep was not a desire to flee a world he didn't like. He was probably not even aware that outside there was a whole human race burdened with pain, threatening and greedy. He surrendered to sleep, naturally, with no inner torment, as to something simple and joyous.

Rafik, on the other hand, was constantly aware of a debased and wretched world, and he'd chosen sleep as a refuge. He only ever felt at ease behind these sheltering walls, barricaded against the fateful presence of beings and things. Around the house lurked a multitude of human wrecks; he couldn't bear their proximity. He remembered with terror the days when he still went out, and his hazardous contacts with the

RAFIK HAD ALWAYS RESPECTED HIS FATHER FOR THE SUPERB ORGANISATION HE PUT INTO LETHARGY AND APATHY

world of men; they were all murderers. He'd retained an inconceivable hatred of them. At a young age, he'd recognised the true worth of the monotonous but sublime existence offered him by his father's home. He owed this security, free of all contingency, to old Hafez, who'd always maintained around him an atmosphere of eternal indolence. Rafik had always respected his father for the superb organisation he put into lethargy and apathy. It was to him he owed the only noble idea he'd ever had of life. And when, at one time, he'd had to sacrifice his love for a woman and submit to his father's will, Rafik had not hesitated, despite the suffering that this sacrifice cost him. Old Hafez had been right. Rafik had realised this and was eternally grateful to him for saving him in time. But now it was old Hafez who was trying to ruin this security so painfully acquired over generations. This appalled Rafik; he felt offended and betrayed.

The woman Rafik had loved, in the days when he still went out, was a young prostitute who lived in a dilapidated old house by the main road. She was known in the neighbourhood as "Imtissal, the students' friend", because she recruited her admirers exclusively among young university students. An entire clientele, barely pubescent, would throng at her door. Rafik would occasionally pay her a visit in the company of other students. In the beginning, Imtissal hardly noticed him; he was a customer like any other. Then she began to treat him differently and refuse the money he gave her. Rafik derived a certain pride from this which led him to believe he was an extraordinary person. Imtissal seemed to experience unusual pleasure when she made love to him. Never had Rafik managed to forget what it had been like, this time of his ferocious discovery of the flesh. Imtissal had set about loving him with fantastic ardour bordering on hysteria. She no longer received her numerous admirers, spent her days waiting for him; she'd become furiously faithful. After some months of this violent passion, Rafik decided he'd marry Imtissal and bring her to live with him in the house.

When he announced his resolution to his father, old Hafez proved adamant; he was categorically against it. He demanded that his son either leave the house or give up his insane plan. Rafik's first reaction was to leave home and marry Imtissal. But they needed money to live on. What could they do? Work! The word was so painful Rafik couldn't even bring himself to utter it. He thought long and hard, agonising between his true passion and the vicissitudes of a life from which sleep and tranquillity would forever be banished. Finally he renounced his love; no joy of the flesh was worth the sacrifice of his peace and quiet. He told Imtissal of his father's opposition; he also confessed his decision to leave her. It was the cause of an unforgettable scene.

This affair had taken place two years earlier, but Rafik had never forgotten the intensity of those erotic moments, the memory of which burned him like a consuming flame. The image of Imtissal haunted him even in his sleep. After their break-up, she'd never wanted to see him again. She'd resumed her old life as a prostitute and the young students came knocking at her door once more.

Rafik kept himself informed of everything she did; he'd learned she had had an illegitimate child and didn't even know who the father was. She was bringing the boy up with her, in her only room, where she made love.

What tormented Rafik most was not his separation from Imtissal, but the misunderstanding that existed between them. Imtissal had grasped only one thing, that Rafik had stopped loving her. He hadn't had time to explain the true reasons for his desertion. She'd immediately called him a pimp, because he'd told her he didn't want to work. Without even trying to listen, she'd screamed like a woman possessed, then thrown him out under a barrage of curses.

Rafik wanted to see her one more time; he'd try to explain to her in detail the beauty of this indolent life that he had preferred to her love. A few days earlier, he'd asked little Hoda to go to her house to beg her to see him. But Hoda had just informed him, before lunch, that this endeavour had failed. Imtissal refused to see him. Since then, Rafik had been considering the only means of approaching Imtissal left to him: to go to her house without warning so she would be forced to listen. He resolved to go out one evening for this purpose. But would she even let him in? He felt anguish at the thought of this meeting. But there was nothing he could do, he had to attempt one final explanation. Perhaps he'd be able to make her understand that he'd never stopped loving her, that it had nothing to do with love, that he was simply incapable of leaving his father's house, this refuge from the ugliness of the world. He'd tell her that all men were murderers, that he was afraid of them. She was sure to think he was mad. What did it matter! At least, after this decisive explanation, he'd feel calmer. Because, since the drama of love had crept between him and his sleep, he hadn't been fully able to enjoy his peace. The ghost of Imtissal, wounded and vindictive, always loomed before him.

Rafik rose from his bed, left the room and crossed the hall. In the kitchen, little Hoda was scuttling about like a mouse; Rafik slipped noiselessly into the dining room. He hadn't lost sight for a moment of his plan to intercept Haga Zohra to stop her seeing his father. For this purpose, the dining room was a good vantage point. Through the door to the hall, which was wide open, Rafik could keep watch over the wooden staircase that led to the floor above. So, should Haga Zohra come, he could hardly miss her. And then there was the sofa; Rafik could stretch out there at the same time as looking out for the odious go-between. He resisted the sofa for the time being; it was still too early, he might immediately fall asleep. He must show some stamina, otherwise his whole laborious manoeuvre would be in vain. Rafik sighed, summoning all the energy of which he was capable. Then he went to the window and looked, through the glass, at the drowsy spectacle of the narrow street. At this hour, everyone in the house opposite was asleep. It was a recent three-storey building, with walls that hadn't been replastered and the unprepossessing appearance of a prison. Rafik had only ever seen men there; the women must be hiding or looking out from behind their closed shutters. These bourgeois families, with their barbaric customs and prejudices, probably didn't allow their women to show themselves out of doors. Rafik thought he'd like to sleep with one of them. But it would be a whole performance and anyway they were bound to be ugly. He abandoned the idea without regret. After a while a boy appeared; he was coming from the direction of the road and playing with a hoop. It was a very heavy iron hoop, and the boy could only just make it roll along the uneven ground. He soon disappeared round the bend of an alley, with shouts of triumph.

Rafik was beginning to feel the ravages of this unwonted vigil; his eyelids were pricking, his legs were starting to go limp. The idea that he was obliged to forego his siesta on account of that accursed Haga Zohra was unbearable torture. This could not go on much longer; in a minute he'd go and lie down on the sofa. With his hands on the window pane and his head spinning, he tensed his muscles, using all his strength to fight off sleep. He felt as if he were swimming upstream in the middle of a river swirling with treacherous eddies. From time to time, with supreme effort, he managed to extricate himself; he raised his head and breathed in deeply. Then he was again sucked down into depths of crushing softness. The waves of an immense, seductive sleep completely submerged him. Once more, he rose to the surface for air. Suddenly a distant noise reached his ears; he thought he was dreaming, shook himself, then listened attentively. The noise became clearer, swelled and turned into the muted rumble of a crowd on the march. Rafik felt it slowly approach, and soon he could see a strange procession filing past the window.

He recognised the man weighed down with chains, followed by a crowd of noisy children.

Some of them were walking backwards in front of him, to get a better view. The man in chains had the build of a giant with long, curly hair that fell to his shoulders. A bushy beard framed his black face streaming with sweat. His torso was bare and he wore a sort of ragged loincloth round his waist. Fragments of old chain were coiled around his ankles, as if to slow his walk and give him an air of pathetic grandeur. He looked like a convict escaped from some imaginary and remote penal colony. With the huge stone he held in his right hand, he struck his chest repeatedly over his heart. The blows came at long intervals and each time he raised his arm, the crowd of children fell silent in anxious expectation. Where the stone came down, his flesh was nothing but a broken, greenish scab. The man punctuated each blow with a stifled groan and incoherent mutterings that sounded like incantations. He was playing the role of penitent sinner with tragic grandeur. Sometimes, through a window, someone would throw him a few coins; the man picked them up and slipped them into a leather pouch that hung at his back.

Rafik had seen him several times before, and as a boy had even followed him on his roamings through the narrow streets. But was this the same man? A great many adopted this practice of spectacular beggary. They formed a fierce sect and prided themselves on the self-inflicted torture they used to move people to pity. Rafik was horrified. The diabolical lengths to which men were reduced in order to live seemed to him the furthest limit of the universal nightmare. The man in chains looked towards the window, slowly lifted his arm and brought the heavy stone down on his chest. In that brief moment, his gaze met that of Rafik, at the window. Rafik closed his eyes and stood still, the man's sharp gaze planted in him like a knife. He waited a long time for the noise of the crowd to subside, then turned away.

Once again there was silence and peace. Rafik felt ill. He was weary, trembling with humiliation and disgust. He instinctively made for the sofa and lay down. The sight of men condemned to the most abject misery depressed him as if he were implicated in their fall. He'd done everything to protect himself from this kind of contact, erected walls between himself and this degraded, submissive humanity. He didn't want any part of such destitution. He felt violated; witnessing such senseless barbarity physically repulsed him. This was real carnage; everywhere the same dazed, busy individuals driven like a herd of buffalo by the same eternal lies.

Rafik breathed loudly, stretched his limbs and tried to forget the horrible stare of the man in chains. Another thing to forget. How long would it take him to forget all these visions of murder perpetrated before his eyes? It was no use hiding, the putrid fumes filtered through the cracks in his hiding place. He remembered that he'd decided to go out to visit Imtissal and felt an irrational fear.

"This will be the last time I go out," he told himself. He stayed still, keeping his ears pricked in devious expectation. There was only silence, an impalpable silence, emptied of all substance. Suddenly, a voice rang out from the floor above. It was old Hafez calling Hoda, and his voice seemed smothered by the monstrous silence. Rafik leapt up, ran to the door and looked down the hall. He saw Hoda who, barefoot, was hurriedly climbing the stairs. Noticing him, the young girl jumped and stopped in her tracks.

"Come here, girl!"

Hoda came back down the stairs and approached him fearfully.

"I know why he's calling you," said Rafik. "He wants to know if Haga Zohra's come yet. You will tell him that she hasn't come and never will. I'm telling you, I'll strangle you if you ever let that woman into the house. What's more, I'm

here, I'm waiting for her."

"It's none of my business," said Hoda. "What's all that got to do with me? Why take it out on me?"

"I know he's promised you money. You want to bring disaster upon us, you horrid girl!"

Hoda was on the verge of tears. She knew how brutal Rafik could be, knew his rude and violent ways. She lowered her eyes, adopted a servile attitude, and resigned herself to the worst.

"I don't want money," she said. "I don't want anything. Did I ask for anything? I do what I'm told."

"Then do what I tell you!" yelled Rafik.

"Be quiet," whispered Hoda." You'll wake everyone up."

Rafik stopped talking, disconcerted by this reminder of the pre-eminence of sleep. He who was usually so careful when it came to respecting other people's slumber! What was happening to him? The exhaustion was probably making him lose control. But there was something else. Rafik realised that he wanted Hoda, and that his desire had been aroused at the very moment she'd whispered to him to be quiet. This silence had an erotic nature, it carried with it traces of oppressive sensuality. He caught Hoda by the neck and tried to drag her towards the sofa.

"Come," he said.

She shook her head and tried to break free.

"Not now," she said. "I don't have time. My master's calling me. I'll come later..."

But Rafik didn't hear her. He gripped her by the waist and pulled her on to him blindly, in a frenzy more for sleep than sensual pleasure. Hoda struggled silently. She knew what to expect: they all behaved like this with her. Rafik was already fumbling under her dress, trying to touch her. She felt his fingers ferreting inside her, a shiver ran through her body, and she fought more vigorously. She had the impression that Rafik was drowning; his movements were feeble and listless. In truth, Rafik was already weary of the struggle. He yawned, his head fell back; his tension was relaxing, he felt himself slide into the depths of unconsciousness. Hoda managed to jerk herself free from his embrace. She rushed up the staircase.

"I'll strangle you, daughter of a whore!"

He waited a moment at the foot of the stairs; now he could hear his father shouting abuse at Hoda for taking so long. Then everything fell back into a heavy and all-enveloping silence. Rafik was still panting in the grip of his frustrated desire; he could no longer feel his legs and his head was spinning, making him giddy. Sleep! But he was too furious with himself to go back and lie down on the sofa. He needed to talk to someone.

V. Serag was not asleep, he was just resting. When Rafik entered the room, he opened his eyes and was astounded to see his brother on his feet at this sacrosanct siesta hour.

"Why are you up? Have you gone mad?"

"I'm not mad," Rafik replied, "it's a lot worse than that. You don't seem to realise. While you're sleeping, I'm the only one dealing with the disaster threatening us."

"What disaster are you talking about?"

"You still haven't understood! It's true, all you think about is roaming the streets. But your father's marriage ought to make you stop and think. It's a calamity that concerns us all. Serag, my brother, our peace is at stake, can't you see?"

"So you really believe in this marriage?"

"Certainly I do. Your father's insisting, if only to annoy us. He hasn't annoyed anyone in a long time; it suddenly came over him. I'm sure he's doing it on purpose."

He sat down on the end of the bed, tucked his legs under him, and buried his face in his hands. The shutters weren't closed and a brilliant light inundated the room. Rafik hated this cold light that enveloped him like a shroud.

"How can you sleep in this light?" he asked.

"I wasn't sleeping," said Serag. "I'm trying to get used to daylight. I don't want to live in the shadows any more."

Rafik sighed and didn't reply. His face in his hands, he appeared to be meditating. He hadn't yet recovered from his struggle with Hoda and a vague excitement lingered inside him. Serag watched him with amused sympathy. He sensed he was fighting off sleep and was curious to see how he'd fare. Could he hold out much longer? He'd never seen his brother make such a tenacious effort to escape the poisonous germs of sleep. It was like a miracle; the miracle of a man suspended above a precipice, held aloft by willpower alone.

"What do you intend to do?"

Rafik uncovered his face, blinked and said sarcastically:

"My being awake at this hour, my dear Serag, is not for pleasure, believe me. I have a plan. The idea is not to let Haga Zohra into the house. Without her help, father will never be able to get married. It's very simple. So, as you can see, I'm waiting for Haga Zohra in order to throw her out."

"So you're going to spend your time waiting for her?"

"Yes, I'll wait for her as long as it takes."

"But that could go on for months."

"Well then! I'll wait for months and even years if necessary."

"You're a hero!" said Serag. "I didn't think you were capable of such sacrifice."

"This sacrifice is going to save our lives," said Rafik. "You can't imagine what it would be like, a woman in our midst. Within a few days, we'd be no better than slaves."

They fell silent. Serag didn't know what to make of his brother's attitude. That this marriage business should have caused Rafik to abandon his siesta seemed madness to him. Something else must be driving him to these extreme lengths. Perhaps it was the hatred he felt towards his father.

"You yourself," he said, "were going to bring a woman into the house, once. Have you forgotten? You've been angry with father ever since your affair with Imtissal."

Rafik gave a start; he seemed suddenly jolted from his torpor. He turned to Serag and glared.

"That's not true," he said, "I'm not angry with him. I realised he was right a long time ago. You don't know how much respect I have for him. I admire him for the kind of life he's led and has given us. He's never wanted to go into business, he's never tried to increase his fortune.

"DON'T LAUGH. IT'S VERY SERIOUS. WE MIGHT BE FORCED TO WORK"

And, most of all, he's always despised other people. All our relatives behaved like servants in front of him, even though some of them were richer. What I've always liked about him is his contempt for worldly matters. That's what we owe this marvellous peace and indolence to. How could I be angry with him? But now he wants to disrupt everything. And I can't allow that."

"I don't see how this marriage will disrupt our life," said Serag.

"How can you not see! This woman will ruin me. A woman wants clothes, jewels, and who knows what else? She might one day think she's possessed by the devil and try to organise an exorcism. Can you see us sleeping in the middle of all those frenzied dancers?"

Serag began to laugh. Rafik's idea struck him as a tremendous joke.

"Don't laugh," said Rafik severely, "it's very serious. Your father might lose his last cent in this affair. We might be forced to work!"

"Fine," said Serag, "I'd be only too pleased."

"Idiot! You'll regret those words."

"I assure you, Rafik, I do want to work."

"You want to work! I'd like to know where you got that idea. You must be either a monster or an idiot. In any case, you don't belong in this family."

"I want to work," said Serag, with an edge of despair. "And leave this house too."

"I swear, you are ungrateful. If you weren't my brother, I'd have let you carry on with this madness. But I feel sorry for you. Which reminds me, what's become of your factory?"

"The factory's still in the same state," Serag replied. "I went to see it again this morning. No one seems to want to finish it."

"So finish it yourself, then," said Rafik. "There's an unusual job. What are you complaining about?"

"You're making fun of me, damn you!"

"Listen, Serag, I'm not making fun of you. I'm just trying to stop you taking the wrong path. Believe me, working is not for you, or any of us."

"Perhaps," said Serag. "But I can't go on living like this."

"You're young. I really feel sorry for you. You don't know what a factory is yet."

"And you do, I suppose?"

"Yes," said Rafik. "When I was studying to be an engineer, they made us visit factories. They were big, unhealthy, sad buildings. I spent the most painful moments of my life there. I've seen the men who worked in these factories; they weren't even men any more. They had misery written all over their faces. The sole reason I gave up my studies was so as not to end up boss of that horde of dying men."

Serag shuddered at this dismal picture. He closed his eyes; he saw his romantic dream of work crumble, disappear into the labyrinth of unfathomable pain. So work could only mean damnation and suffering. Serag said nothing, prey to a dull anxiety.

There was a long silence, then they heard a slight creaking sound. Rafik jumped off the bed, opened the door and glanced into the hall.

"No," he said, "there's no one there."

"Did you think it was Haga Zohra?"

"Yes, I thought it was her. Never mind! I have to move, otherwise I'll fall asleep. What misery! And I can't count on any of you. Your brother Galal's sleeping like a baby. He's still not really aware of the catastrophe hanging over him. But soon he won't be able to sleep any more."

"How are you going to stop him sleeping?" said Serag. "Nothing can wake Galal. Anyway, I don't believe he's still thinking about this business. He's probably already forgotten it."

"He won't forget for long," said Rafik. "I'm fed up with watching him calmly relaxing, while I'm killing myself keeping watch. He'll have to help me."

"By Allah! I can't see Galal leaving his bed to lie in wait for Haga Zohra. You're mad even to think of it."

"I'll drag him out of his bed, believe me. He hasn't grasped the implications of this fatal marriage yet. When he realises, he won't be sleeping either."

Rafik began to pace the room; every now and then he'd stop by the window. Serag's room was at the rear of the house, it looked over a wasteland where thin shrubs grew amid all kinds of rubbish.

In the middle of the wasteland was a dwarf palm tree, withered and barren, where people came to answer the call of nature. At that moment, a squatting child, his galabieh pulled up over his private parts, was gloomily relieving himself. Further on, the sinuous line of houses was visible across the fields. Rafik was happy; he'd just rid Serag of his illusions. He'd have liked to put him off the idea of work for good; it would be doing him an invaluable service. All his abhorrence of people's busy lives had risen to his throat. He turned round and said with malicious cruelty:

"Do you know, my dear Serag, there are countries where men wake up at four o'clock in the morning to go and work in the mines?"

"The mines!" said Serag. "It's not true, you're trying to scare me."

He was deeply distressed. This alarming conception of work with which Rafik was inoculating him, drop by drop, like a poison, was beginning to seem like the truth. He'd have liked to find out more, but Rafik had stopped speaking and resumed his pacing.

"Tell me, Rafik, my brother, it's not true what you just said?"

"What was that?"

"That in some countries the men wake up at four o'clock in the morning to go and work in the mines."

"It's true," said Rafik. "We don't have mines here yet, but it'll happen. They'll discover some. They'll discover anything to force men to work and make beasts of them."

"But isn't it possible to work any other way?"

Rafik laughed sharply. It amused him to see Serag frightened as a child.

"Don't be scared. There aren't any mines here yet. But men are capable of anything. They'll find a way to discover mines, even where there aren't any."

"Who told you that?"

"Nobody. But I know men better than you do. I tell you, it won't take them long to ruin this fertile valley and turn it into a hellhole. That's what they call progress. Haven't you ever heard that word? Well, you might as well know, when a man starts talking to you about progress, he wants to make you his slave. In any case, for the time being, we have this magnificent security surrounding us. And you want to get away from it! You're crazy, you don't know what's in store for you."

Rafik had stopped again in front of the window. He said nothing, he was looking at the diminutive palm tree, which was wearily swaying its leaves. The child had gone, and a man advanced in years, wearing a turban, had taken his place. He seemed to have settled in for good, gazing into the distance, desperately immobile. He personified the image of humanity itself, squatting and happy in its excrement. Rafik turned away and came back to the bed.

"Listen, I was asking during lunch what news you'd brought us from outside. Actually, I wanted to know the atmospheric conditions. Is it very cold? Is there a lot of dust about?"

"Why all these questions?"

"I have to go out," said Rafik. "But I haven't quite made up my mind yet. It's only an idea."

Serag looked at his brother in bewilderment.

"You, Rafik, you're going out?"

"Yes, I'm going out. But, believe me, it's not to go looking for work. And now, sleep well; I'm off to try to save us from disaster."

He left the room and went back to the dining room. He was still preoccupied with the same idea: preventing Haga Zohra from seeing his father. He lay down on the sofa and waited. He did not wait long. Sleep fell on him like a lead weight and crushed him. ◉

The illustrations for this piece are available to purchase as a limited edition of 50 signed and numbered lino-cuts, priced at £50 each. To place an order please email mireillefau@hotmail.com

Across
Enemy
Lines

A SHORT STORY BY RJ GHORBANI.

Leaving the house that weekday morning, after a brief sleep punctured by the sound of propellers, she felt confident that radio rumours of cancellation would prove unfounded. Through snipers' eyes, she ventured, dogless, through the quotidian fields, fingers finding security in the laminated resident's identity pass that would allow her back home. Trampling the scorched earth of the disbanded peace camp, Hannah thought of the villagers who had salved their consciences with a polite ramble—hardly a "march" —around the capital the previous weekend. Their Volvos were now replete with "Make poverty history" stickers, which exempted them from further dissent. She wondered what they would make of today's proceedings.

Over the brow of the hill, the radius of calm around the hotel caused lingering doubts to resurface, but a gust of activity to the left reassured her that the march would be happening as planned. Circus colours pulled her closer, leaping over the last patch of grass to pick a path onto the narrow high street, where vibrant visitors swilled from coaches along the low walls and music from a dynamo-powered machine pebble-dashed cottages with sound. Conspicuously bland in second hand shoes and clothes, Hannah wrapped herself in carnival camouflage and moved in time.

Frivolity oozed from the park, gaining momentum as it travelled and solidifying into seriousness on the surfaces it touched; faces distorted into caricature as effigies of leaders looked down with malign intent, and phrases hardened onto placards as slogans urged the world to re-imagine itself. In the ideas of interlopers, Hannah found validation; in the smiles of outsiders, she found solidarity. In this way they travelled, watched from the undergrowth, until steps foundered and voices loudened.

Half way to the hotel, the route was blocked by a steel barrier, its rectangular mesh open enough to allow a shallow view of the police people waiting beyond, black helmets and rubber boots clashing with the aggressive fluorescence of their jackets. Separated by a metal fence, a uniform and an attitude, one group of humans faced another and waited.

The music pedlar still peddled and the sound still travelled, over the heads of the police people. On the right side of the fence, someone tried to reason through the bars, to explain the logic of their cause, to gain access to those responsible. Evacuated of opinion, the cordon stood firm against them.

Someone threw a banana into the enclosure, reducing ciphers of authority to caged beasts, and everyone laughed. Then, someone remembered why they were there and began chanting words for the leaders to hear. Softly at first, inaudible until more voices were added, the words contained the evils of the world, the poverty and squalor, the misery and death. Those who uttered them seized power for those who had none and, for a time, they felt emboldened. Hannah tried to guess the length of the driveway and the distance their sentiments would have to travel.

When none of the leaders had emerged to listen and nothing in the world had changed, the words became inflamed. Ignited by injustice, they wrapped themselves in soft bodies and hurled themselves at the fence. With indignation as their battering ram, human projectiles held hands to swell the metal inwards in their shape.

The slotted triangles held firm against them until sentience kicked in. Then, the first panel was lifted from its socket, pulled free with laughable ease, and sent surfing over the top to show their displeasure. In no time at all, the barrier was reduced to a flimsy screen, held up only by the determination of gloved fingers. Sensing danger, the markings of the front line changed from yellow to black.

Carried on the tide of surging bodies, Hannah found herself at the fence, scanning the line of smoked visors, blinking at her fellow creatures in disbelief. An impulse too compelling to interrogate caused her to trawl the identity parade with renewed interest and, sure enough, five bodies from the right, she found the rigid figure of Davey Sharpe and the secondary school of a distant town. The initials on his uniform told her he had never left.

Suddenly, his lack of teenage popularity made sense, grounding him for his future profession, and Hannah remembered the gauntlet of taunts she had crossed to befriend him, rescuing him from obscurity to embark on the adventures of adolescence. Lagging behind their burgeoning bodies, their minds had struggled to understand what was happening as her rebellion flailed uncontrollably and his conformity was born. Only now, with the abyss of adulthood between them, did their youthful trajectories make sense, landing them on either side of a tenuous metal fence.

Hannah positioned herself in front of the broad-shouldered emblem of her youth and thought she saw a flicker of recognition. But, before they could take stock of their relative positions, the fence began to move. On an unseen pivot, the metal

"...AND NOTHING IN THE WORLD HAD CHANGED."

grille swung into the protest, ploughing people as it travelled and closing off the way they had come.

As she turned to flee, Hannah saw Davey locking clear perspex shields with his colleagues. Behind them, another row was arranged like the scalloped edges of an ornamental garden and, behind them, another flanked by horses. With the fence discarded, the police people advanced, taking advantage of the scuffle to press their orders into her back. An incongruous voice, mangled by plastic, sounded from behind. "I can get you out of here," it offered, straining under misplaced camaraderie.

Without looking back, Hannah felt the lifetime inscribed in the transparent force field between them, the years in which opinions had diverged and crystallised. She considered the legacy of a friendship destined never to be made, and mourned the conversations they had never had. With the defiance of a safe passage home already in her pocket, Hannah linked arms with those around her and walked with them, ten abreast.

Herded into a slim lane, they were offered a new perspective, of open fields and elevated platforms. From high above, television cameras recorded every move, making them actors in a performance that was every bit as stage-managed as the speeches of their leaders would be, and mocking them in their failed endeavour to hold those men to account. 🐚

PRACTICAL
IDLER

ST DEINIOLS

In the first of a regular series, Robert Wringham visits a residential library

The best sort of library plays host to everything the urban flâneur holds dear: peace and quiet, dog-eared books, crackly old jazz records, fascinating characters lurking in every corner and haphazard furnishings liberated from closed-down gentleman's clubs. Today's library directors are forced to go the extra mile to make these oases all the more appealing: the daily papers are laid out ready for you; access is granted to the Internet; librarians are getting younger and more attractive and it's all absolutely free. Many public libraries are even installing coffee and tea facilities for their punters. No wonder Ray Bradbury described them as "birthing places of the universe". All we need now are on-site tobacconists and somewhere to get some shut-eye and we need not ever bother going home.

That's precisely the idea behind Saint Deiniol's library in the leafy town of Hawarden in Wales: it's the only library in the UK to have bedrooms. Not only is the library (of 230,000 theology, philosophy and history books) housed in a beautiful and rambling nineteenth-century country house; you can also stay the night there —or even a month. That's right: it's a residential library. For a relatively low sum of money you have your own bibliographic retreat at which you can make full use of the collection; have dinner; sleep in a proper bed and wake up to enjoy a continental breakfast. Heaven on earth, surely.

They even have a copy of Johnson's *Idler* in the annexe. To think that people pay so much money to go to health spas.

The library was put together by Victorian politician and dedicated polymath, William E. Gladstone (though the current building wasn't erected until after his death, as a publicly-funded memorial). Gladstone was probably an enemy of idleness: he was the holder of three first-class university degrees, curator of this great library, self-stated utilitarian, staunchly religious, four times Prime Minister of Britain and it seems that (for a spell during his early years) he opposed the abolition of slavery and factory legislation. Phew. He even personally delivered many of the books from his private residence to a publicly accessible building by wheelbarrow, shortly after his eightieth birthday. Nonetheless, you can't help but admire the guy's gung-ho spirit and his ability to stick in the craw of Queen Victoria who once remarked upon his insolent lack of formality in her presence.

Why exactly Gladstone chose to erect the only residential library in Britain rather than a regular non-residential one remains something of a mystery but James Cape Story (a regular Saint Deiniol's patron circa 1905) was right in declaring the library, "a place for restful meditation, for research, for mental and spiritual refreshment". It's just the place for an idler's retreat. ◉

www.st-deiniols.org

IDLER'S RETREAT: ST
DEINIOL'S RESIDENTIAL
LIBRARY HAS ROOMS
FROM £22 A NIGHT

STOP THE WAR: STAY IN THE GARDEN

Faced with a case of activist burnout, Graham Burnett decided to get off the streets and into his own back yard

I guess that we are all familiar with the saying "think globally, act locally". Despite this, we often still tend to be REactive rather than PROactive to what is happening in the world around us. I believe that this is something our society and media encourages. Think of the mainstream press and TV soap operas or reality shows. They thrive on despair, gossip and confrontation—"if it bleeds it leads", as the old Fleet Street saying goes. A constant stream of bad news and car crash entertainment taps into our negative fixations and has a cumulatively dis-empowering effect on us. We learn that blaming and complaining, like living on a diet of junk food, offers short term pay-offs that might fill the empty gaps in our lives for a while but in the long run don't actually make us feel satisfied in a good way. In the meantime, we have avoided taking responsibility for our own part in making real change happen.

Things aren't too different in the worlds of politics—the main parties often seem more interested in rivalries, posturing and short-term vote grabbing than in focusing on real solutions to social conflicts and environmental threats. The Native American Navaho people taught that when planning for the future, we should always think at least seven generations ahead. Yet I'm hard pressed to recall a recent politician who looks much more than seven *days* past their own tabloid-friendly sound bites and spin...

For my own part, I became involved in protest and campaigning activities during the late 1970s. As a youth aware enough to realise that Labour wasn't working, the Tories would only ever work for their own class and that the National Front were a Nazi front, organisations like Rock Against Racism and the Anti Nazi League offered the answers I sought. I also became politicised by the raucous punk of bands such as The Clash, The Ruts, Gang of 4 and Crass.

Shortly afterwards I also became involved with animal rights groups such

I WAS BEGINNING TO
FEEL DESPONDENT,
CYNICAL AND
CONVINCED THAT
NOTHING COULD
GET BETTER

as the Hunt Saboteurs and various Anti-Vivisec-tion organisations, and throughout the eighties and up until the mid nineties I was a regular at meetings, pickets, protests and demonstrations: Ban the Bomb, Stop the War, Smash the Poll Tax, Boycott Shell, Oppose the Criminal Justice Act, No to GM crops, Wreck the Road Building pro-gram and so on and on... Notice the pattern yet? Like so many radically motivated and socially concerned people, my focus was almost exclusively on *stopping* rather than *starting*. Don't get me wrong, protest and resistance movements are of course vital in raising awareness as well as advancing and protecting our rights and freedoms, and their importance and value should never be underplayed or dismissed. Besides which the big CND or Anti-Apartheid rallies were always a good place to meet up with friends and acquaintances... But for me personally I had begun to feel that I was defining myself more in negative terms of what I was Against rather than what I was positively For. I was also beginning to feel the symptoms of "activist burnout"—despondent, cynical, convinced that nothing can get better and not wanting to know when it actually did. The problem with being a part of a permanent "culture of opposition" is that whether we won or lost on any particular issue, "they" always had the next struggle lined up for us. The next social injustice, the next war, the next law. And always in "their" terms, in "their" arena...

I had reached a point where I needed to think in terms of solu-tions rather than problems. About this time I was reminded of a little Sufi story I'd read some years earlier;

Late one evening an innkeeper walked into the main guestroom now lit by several oil lamps. One of the guests is peering under tables and into corners obviously looking for something.

"What have you lost?" asked the innkeeper.

"My purse", replies the guest, pushing a bench aside to look underneath.

"Do you know roughly where you lost it?"

"Yes, in the garden"

"Then why on earth are you looking for it in here?"

The guest grunts, heaving at a heavy piece of furniture. "This is where the light is," and continues the search.

For me maybe it was time to get back to the garden. Bill Mol-lison, the co-founder of the Permaculture movement, once said that: *"You start with your nose, then your hands, your back door, your doorstep. You get all that right, then everything is right. If all that's wrong, nothing can ever be right"*. Paradoxically it seems that the more we focus our positive energies and time on the things in our lives that we can affect directly, rather than on those where we can make no real difference, the greater and wider our "circles of influence" actually become, expanding outwards and creating opportunities to make ever bigger changes.

During the mid 1990s my friend Stella lived on a housing estate in south east London. Like so much of the inner city, this area was blighted by poverty, crime, poor transport links, lack of green spaces and vandalism. However Stella had a belief in the abilities of ordinary people to make a difference, and started at the end of her own nose. She planted up a small wooden box of flowers on the window ledge of her flat to add a splash of colour to the street. Some of her neighbours informed her that she was wasting her time, and sure enough, by the next day the box was smashed up and the flowers were strewn and trampled across the pavement. So she replaced it with another window box. And exactly the same thing happened again. So she replaced it with another. And exactly the same thing happened again. So she replaced it with another. And this time something interesting happened. A box of bright marigolds, petunias and geraniums appeared on the ledge of the house across the street. Then another a little further down the road. Soon window boxes, tubs and containers of flowers and herbs began to pop up all over the estate. People began to talk to each other, and from the confidence gained from these small beginnings grew Green Adventure, a multicultural urban regeneration project that encompassed a vegetable box delivery scheme, food growing initiatives, a Local Exchange Trading System (LETS), a bicycle trailer building and repair workshop, play schemes, educational and employment projects and forest gardens and community orchards. Stella decided to be a model rather than a critic, and never let anybody tell her that an individual can't make a difference.

As another famous world-changer called Martin Luther King once put it, *"even if I knew that tomorrow the world would go to pieces, I would still plant my apple tree..."* 🌀

Graham Burnett is a permaculture teacher, designer and author of 'Permaculture a Beginner's Guide' and 'Earth Writings'. For more information see www.spiralseed.co.uk

HOME BREW

It's time to rediscover the art of making your own beer, says Pete Brown

We kept it in the airing cupboard. I remember cans of syrup and endless stirring. Then the airing cupboard. I'd go and look at it every now and again, hoping it would do something. It never did. My dad and I never knew why.

After a week or so we'd try it. It was the right colour for lager. It tasted vaguely alcoholic. But the whole 40 litre container was flat and lifeless. We'd drink a couple of pints, try to persuade each other that it tasted vaguely of beer, then the rest would sit there, until we poured it away and tried again.

Now that I know a lot about beer, I can appreciate just how blindly Dad and me, and tens of thousands of whiskery blokes, were stumbling through the home brew boom of the 1970s and 1980s. A basic understanding of the brewing process lets you see immediately what we were doing wrong. And it allows you to brew beers that equal, even exceed, the standards of anything available on the bar down your local.

In medieval Britain households were largely self-sufficient. Every self-respecting peasant kitchen brewed beer just as it baked bread. It took centuries of gradual osmosis for the more talented of these home brewers to transform into the handful of brewing giants we know today. This transition was completed by the 1880 Inland Revenue Act. Concern that somebody somewhere might be drinking beer that wasn't served with a big slice of tax revenue impelled the government to insist that this natural, timeless process—a process that had kept the population alive for centuries when drinking plain water would have resulted in dysentery, and when beer was the most reliable source of vitamins and nutrients—could only be permitted upon purchase of a five guinea licence. The art of brewing at home was lost.

The United States had it worse. Prohibition banned the production of any alcohol, in any fashion (to paraphrase Bill Hicks: if you make a process that happens in nature illegal, aren't you saying that God made a mistake?). In 1933 when Prohibition was repealed, a clerical error meant the words "and/or beer" were accidentally omitted from the bit that said people were allowed to make wine at home. No one in government had the time to correct this oversight, and home brewing remained illegal until 1979.

Back in the UK we had a head start—the 1880 licence condition was abolished in 1963. But we exercised our new found freedom to brew in a very modern way. Why go to all the trouble of understanding the delicate interplay of grain, yeast and spiky little flower when you could buy a kit from Boots and just add water? British home brewing was the alcoholic equivalent of the Pot Noodle.

The only good thing enthusiasts had to say about their issue was that it only cost them 3p a pint. Their guests would silently fume that at this price, they had been fleeced.

When they got their turn, the Americans approached brewing in a completely different way. By 1979 the only beers commercially available were so uniformly bland and tasteless that Budweiser was considered a premium brand. People who had visited Europe and sampled more characterful brews were keen to create an alternative at home.

"Home brewing here is not about getting cheap beer and beating taxes," says the splendidly-named Randy Mosher, one of the leading exponents of the craft. "People try to make interesting recipes, or to brew 'clone brews', getting as close as they can to established classic beer recipes. It's about getting better as a brewer, and it's about winning awards for your beer."

America today boasts 250,000 active home brewers. In the early eighties some amateurs moved out of their garages and turned pro, offering the first domestically brewed alternative to Bud-style lagers for seventy years. As the commercial craft beer market celebrates its quarter century, it's growing at ten per cent year on year while the big brands suffer long term decline. Beers like Samuel Adams, Brooklyn Lager and Goose Island IPA are increasingly available in the UK, where their heady but fresh, citrusy characters rival the very best traditional British ales.

While the Americans were changing their perceptions of what beer could be, British home brewing fell into decline. Boots stopped selling home brew kits about fifteen years ago. "There used to be three home brew magazines on the shelves of WH Smiths. There are none now," says James McCrorie of the UK's Craft Brewing Association, "It wasn't just people's knowledge. The standard of ingredients available was pathetic. If

you were lucky those kits produced alcoholic Tizer."

McCrorie founded the Craft Brewing Association in the mid-1990s to provide a focal point for rediscovering and propagating a lost art. Suppliers got in touch and made quality ingredients and kit readily available. People swapped tips. By the end of the decade, British amateur brewers were having their ales appraised favourably by the professionals at the Great British Beer Festival. Just like the US, a steady stream of enthusiasts have joined the scores of new commercial breweries now opening across Britain.

The process of brewing is simple to understand, but requires focus and discipline if you're going to do it well. Alcohol is produced when yeast attacks fermentable sugars—either from grapes, the starch inside grain, or commercially produced sugar or syrup. So in classic brewing, grain is "mashed"—boiled for a couple of hours to get the sugars out—to produce a sweet, sticky brew. Hops are added to provide bitterness and balance, then the yeast is introduced to do its thing.

Given that it arguably has the cushiest job of any living organism—eating sugar, pissing and farting alcohol and carbon dioxide—yeast can be surprisingly temperamental and moody. Ale yeasts prefer to ferment at room temperature, whereas lager yeasts will only get to work at very cool temperatures. Ale yeasts work quicker so you'll get finished beer in a week; lager ideally wants about four weeks. Understand this process, and you can start to appreciate why boiling the kettle and adding hot water bit by bit to a can of syrup, then sticking the whole lot in a very warm place for a couple of weeks, was never going to produce anything recognisable as beer.

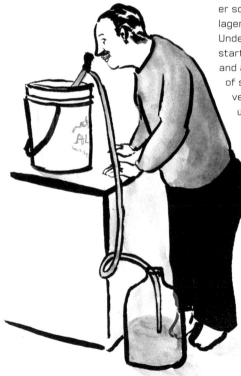

Better quality kits through specialist suppliers are still popular. Kits are how most craft brewers still get started. Follow the process carefully, keep your equipment sterile, and you can produce passable versions of classic beers for around 16p a pint.

But price is not the main motivation for the true craft brewer. True acolytes spurn kits for mini-mash tuns and fermenters, following the same process as commercial brewers in their sheds and cellars. They're creating beer styles that are not commercially available in

Britain, digging into the history of brewing to recreate beers such as strong Victorian India Pale Ales. Brupaks is a company that provides over twenty malt varieties, twenty-five hop varieties and more than twenty different yeast strains to the amateur brewer. "This is far wider than any brewery inventory and allows us to brew some of the most interesting beers in Britain," claims McCrorie.

Some hardcore home brewers insist that Britain is turning into a beer desert commercially; that we are faced with a dwindling choice of identical brands. This might be true in high street drinking sheds, but it strikes an odd note at a time when, if you know where to look, there is a richer diversity of beer more readily available than ever before. Nevertheless, modern craft brewing offers the intriguing opportunity for the idler to create these beers himself—and even nudge them to his own tastes. You want it more bitter? Stronger? Lighter? Once you know what you're doing, it's up to you. In your kitchen, you can re-forge the links with natural processes and ingredients that our ancestors took for granted.

And, yes, 16p a pint does hold out a certain appeal. 🦪

Find out how to get started by talking to the people at www.craftbrewing.org.uk Get top quality ingredients and equipment from www.brupacks.com Pete Brown's Three Sheets to the Wind: One Man's Quest for the Meaning of Beer is out now.

Cheers!

HOW TO BUILD A TREEHOUSE

The trick is to raise bodgemanship to the level of an artform, says Robert Twigger

I have found treehouse building to be a shortlived but demanding occupation not unlike sandcastle building with wood and nails, and in the air not on the ground. You should not plan too much. You should not use new wood. I did. It looks bad, all white and planed and soft up there next to the much better old stuff I gleaned from a broken fence and out of a skip. Treehouse building is not for the fainthearted, or rather, it is, or could be, as long as you go step by step. Using three trees close together is easier than building a platform that encircles one. Expect lots of squeaks and groans when the wind blows. Do not envisage lofty domains in the sky. OK, I know there are many protesters out there who have built huge skyworthy treehouses but I am not among them. I am an ordinary Dad type guy with a handful of nails and a borrowed handsaw. NO POWER TOOLS ALLOWED. This I think has something of the status of a law about it. Power tools, spirit levels, plum bobs, rulers and measures of any kind are OUT. You have to rely solely on the eye. Let me expand: if you use measures and spirit levels, the building proceeds too slowly. It becomes a tedious job. The aim, instead, is to achieve by lunchtime what you only half imagined at breakfast. Take my favourite feature—the balcony or verandah in the sky. Mine came about only because I didn't want to cut off off some long pieces of wood sticking out at the front of the treehouse. These sticking out bits suggested a balcony and very quickly I built one. It was here that I learnt to treat wood as a dry stone waller treats, er, dry stone. Search through your pile of wood for bits that seem to fit. You will be absolutely amazed at the serendipity at work in treehouse building. Often a piece you chopped off and were prepared to discard is exactly the right size for some awkward gap next to the window. Bodgemanship or what the French call *bricolage*, is raised to the level of an artform, indeed, at the

risk of drawing scornful comments upon myself, I'd say that treehouse building is a kind of modern-primitive installation sculpture practiced by frustrated architects. And it's much cheaper and far more fun than having an extension built on your suburban semi.

I was inspired by Japanese carpenters who rely mostly on the eye and avoid using instruments that measure length and levelness. So far I only used the spirit level on the base platform and I am very glad I did as it is satisfyingly flat whereas everything else is a bit wobbly and off kilter. OK, you can use the spirit level for the very important bits but not for unimportant things like planking the walls etc. I think nails are best as you can move fast. It's good for the treehouse to grow quickly, especially if there are others waiting around to use it.

This is my first treehouse for thirty years. I could use it as a great nature viewing platform or simply as a place to spy on the neighbours. Or read books up there and sip a gin and tonic as the sun goes down. Treehouses are for adults. Be extravagant in the design. Overengineer using lots of wood. Ask any old man serving at B&Q where to buy used wood, they'll know. Theoretically, the sky's the limit, or at least the top branches are. I stupidly encouraged the children to believe a crow's nest high in the highest leaves would be forthcoming. It's possible—but it will have to wait until next year.

More tips: The accidental balcony or deck that extends like a prow out of the front of the treehouse has proved to be abidingly popular. So has the trapdoor and ropeladder. Don't be averse to nailing directly into the treetrunks—it's much easier that way and the tree survives even if it is screaming at some frequency inaudible to humans. I made the mistake of making the first roof too low. The kids and I were bent over eating our sandwiches up there like Gulliver in a Lilliputian pub. High ceilings if possible please! The solution was simple—just tear that low roof off. The sculpture paradigm rather than the building paradigm means you are allowed to make mistakes, change things, tear them off and start again. We raised the ceiling and put a flat roof unconnected to the walls high above the platform, kind of like a Malay house where there is a gap all around between the roof and the tops of the walls. This acts like a continuous window.

Just thinking about the treehouse every morning before I got up was exciting—that was another great discovery—having this ongoing adventure happening in the back-garden. Naming the place was important too. My seven year old son suggested "The Treehouse of Happiness". We painted a sign and hung it over the door. It was the best thing I did all summer. ◉

Robert Twigger has a website, roberttwigger.com. His latest book is called Voyageur

MEMORANDA

KENNEY
A CARNIVAL OF REVOLUTION
SHARP Part Two
The Politics of SUBVERSION
we are everywhere
Yvon Le Bot
YA BASTA!
THE ZAPATISTAS
GLOBALIZE LIBERATION
CITY LIGHTS
Restructuring and Resistance Diverse voices of struggle in Western Europe
MULTITUDE
WAR AND DEMOCRACY IN THE AGE OF EMPIRE
PARA PRINCIPIANTES
E. Adamovsky • Ilustradores Unidos
James M. Jasper
The Art of Moral Protest
Rebecca Solnit
NO LOGO
NAOMI KLEIN
FLAMINGO
NAOMI KLEIN
FENCES AND WINDOWS
VINTAGE CANADA
REBEL
SIAMO DAPPERTUTTO
STEPHEN DUNCOMBE
CULTURAL RESISTANCE READER
Direct Action and Liberal Democracy
April Carter
ANARCHISM A Very Short Introduction
John Quail The Slow Burning Fuse
PRINCE PETR KROPOTKIN
MUTUAL AID
John Rety
ABOUT ANARCHISM
NICOLAS WALTER
THROUGH THE ANARCHIST PRESS
Bayer Anarchism & Violence
BLECHMAN
REVOLUTIONARY ROMANTICISM
ORGASMS OF HISTORY
Yves Fremion
The MURRAY BOOKCHIN Reader
Edited by Janet Biehl
Bookchin
Post-Scarcity Anarchism
From Urbanization to Cities
Bookchin
PORTUGAL • THE IMPOSSIBLE REVOLUTION? • PHIL MAILER
Sam Dolgoff
GRAHAM PURCHASE Evolution & Revolution
PREPARING FOR NONVIOLENT DIRECT ACTION
GRANNY MADE ME AN ANARCHIST
STUART CHRISTIE

BOOKSHELF

JOHN JORDAN

Picture by John Jordan

ROOTS READING

Tony White visits News From Nowhere, Liverpool's radical bookshop

Liverpool's independent and activist bookshop, News from Nowhere, nestles comfortably amongst the non-chainstore surroundings of Bold Street in the city centre. They've been going for 32 years. Mandy who is part of the non-profit workers' co-operative that runs the shop tells the *Idler* that the fact they have survived so long is "testament to Liverpool's radicalism."

Alongside the shop's bread-and-butter titles, the big-selling books by Chomsky, Billy Bragg or Mark Thomas, News from Nowhere also stock a wide range of independent books. Mandy picked out a few of the current crop for the *Idler*.

"In terms of protest *as such*, these are current books that come out of the idea that 'the personal is political', which is very much our ethos. So when you look at life and politics in that way, you can't separate your personal life from the wider picture—

so working for change in small ways, for example addressing change in your own life is as important as working on a macro level to *change the world*."

Naming the Dead: A Serious Crime, Maya Anne Evans.

Maya Anne Evans was the first person to go to court for "participating in an unauthorised demonstration in the vicinity of Parliament" under the new Serious Organised Crime and Police Act. Her crime? Reading aloud the names of all the British Soldiers killed in the Iraq war. This is her account of why she felt moved to act against both an "unjust law and an unjust war."

Justice Not Vengance, £7.00

How Not to Teach: the Diary of an Urban Primary Teacher, Mr Read

"I think Mr Read is a pseudonym—he's probably still teaching," Mandy tells me.

Written by a Merseyside teacher, this book is an indictment of the current education system in both policy and practice: the whole nightmare of SATs, league-tables and targets, the government initiatives, the targets and strategies that take all of the joy out of teaching and waste our children's lives. "This is a good one for the *Idler*," Mandy suggests, "because it demonstrates that it's sometimes better to do nothing at all than to do damage."
Continuum, £12.99

Enough Blood Shed: 101 Solutions to Violence, Terror and War, Mary-Wynne Ashford
"This should be required reading for every politician—if even one of these solutions might work then it's worth it." The 101 solutions include the old Quaker saying "speak truth to power", and the book is notable for its suggestion that there are currently two global superpowers: one being the United States of America, the other, perhaps surprisingly, "world public opinion".
New Society Publishers, £13.50

News From Nowhere Radical & Community Bookshop:
96 Bold Street, Liverpool L1 4HY
www.newsfromnowhere.org.uk

" AND THESE ONES ~~AR~~ HERE ARE THE ANTI-HUNT PROTESTERS "

By Jonathan Pugh

FANTASY FICTION

Tony White on Steve Beard's scary new novel

"Whatever you do, don't mention Diana." Steve Beard's new novel *Meat Puppet Cabaret* opens with a tame journalist being reminded of the deal he struck to get an interview with King Charles III, exiled to geostationary orbit in the Ark of Old England, following a coup by Prince, now "Cheikh", William who, meanwhile, has established the Islamic Republic of New New England back on Earth. It's a deal that proves impossible to stick to however, and once in the presence of Charles the hack just can't help himself: "Some say that Diana was eight months pregnant when she died. What is your comment?" This is when things really fall apart, and the reader joins a blasphemous cast of characters trapped in a narrative loop of computer games and twisted anthropology.

Allegra (Diana's daughter, born by emergency c-section in that wrecked Mercedes in Paris), John Dee, Jack the Ripper, some gender-reassigned Kray-twin analogues and a variety of African deities are drawn in to a series of ritual repetitions and game-plays, via Parliament Hill, pornographic cut-ups and several other universes, in search of an occult procedure that might enable some kind of access to, or understanding of, exactly what happened in the few minutes before and after the crash. But nothing is going to be that simple. *Meat Puppet Cabaret* is a scary *tour-de-force* that pulls the curtains away from the media and psychic dominance of the Diana myth ("that insufferable expression of piety and need on her smiling docile face") and nags away at you for weeks until you finally have no choice but to pick it up and read it again. 🎧

Steve Beard, Meat Puppet Cabaret, *Raw Dog Screaming Press, £15.99*

ANTIGUA

Young man about town Ed Cumming finds a more sophisticated way of life hiding behind paradise

In many people's heads a place like Antigua (one of the first things local Caribbeans will concede is that their individually lovely countries share a lot of characteristics) represents the idler's dream working environment—the national motto is "land of sea and sun" which is, all things considered, not a bad to place to start. Yet it is a country of two distinct halves, and these parts throw up interesting contrasts and revelations about the nature of work both on the island and, by contrast, in Britain and the States. On the one hand you have the developments around the coast, where laziness is not so much expected as required of the thousands of tourists who make the trip from Britain and the US to enjoy a week or a fortnight of essential relaxation, and then on the other you have the day to day existence of the Antiguans, who have to survive in this warm, gentle paradise that others are prepared to pay so much to visit.

The image of many outsiders is that as a nation, the Caribbean has a relaxed work ethic, an image created and perpetuated by holiday brochures, Lilt adverts and cricket coverage which depict a world of steel bands, hammocks and natives passing the day sitting in the sunshine, conversing with their neighbours and arguing about the various problems of the government. When you get a taxi from the airport, your driver enthusiastically tells you all about how friendly and relaxed the place is, and how everyone who comes here falls in love with it, it's difficult not to think that this is just the speech he performs to all of his visitors—if nothing else Antiguans are acutely aware that their livelihoods depend on the constant influx of foreign money—but scratch the surface and it becomes clear that this culture of "liming", or chilling out, runs much deeper than the swimming pool at Sandals.

The first thing you notice is that nothing is done in a hurry. An arranged meeting for four o'clock will happen any time after five, a plumber scheduled to come on a certain day might come then, but then again might come the next day, depending on what he has to do, and though this is frustrating initially, quickly you realise that it is simply normality. Once you accept that it's how people behave, you start acting the same way, and you find that it's received as entirely natural. They call it "island time", but really it is a way of thinking which refuses to play by go-faster Western expectations of punctuality and efficiency, and has its payback in the quality of the work done. The plumber who comes a day late will stay until his job's done, and it will be done properly. Contrast this to the equivalent workman in Britain, who might come on time but will then have to leave without finishing the task, and come back

"As one local tour operator, who worked for five years in New York put it, 'in the States
you live to work, but here you work to live'"

in a fortnight, depending on how busy he is.

The second thing which becomes evident is that for the most part people don't work hours nearly as long as they do in Britain. If they want to go to the beach for the day, or simply hang out, they will. Work takes a back seat. The explanation for all of this becomes very clear when you speak to anyone who lives here, and in comparison to our hyperactive society at home it is simply a matter of perspective. As one local boat tour operator, who worked for five years in New York, put it, "in the States you live to work, but here you work to live", which despite being an

oversimplification of the issue encompasses so much of what we put up with at home—we have lost sight of the purpose of work, which is fundamentally to put food on the table and a roof over our heads. By comparison, once these basics are satisfied, so are many Antiguans. In the year-round good weather and prevailing closeness of community, people know that they have all they need for a good, full life all around them, without iPods and running machines and elaborate cosmetics. Money facilitates, but does not dominate, which is interesting because it provides a rebuff to the usual riposte of anti-idlers back home that it's essentially for people with means, people who can afford to work in "paroxysms of diligence" rather than full-time, complacent middle-classes looking for intellectual justification to sit around all day. Antigua, aside from the big hotels, is basically Third World. An average wage is around 100 East Caribbean Dollars a day, equivalent to about twenty two pounds. This is scarcely compensated by the cost of living, which is ultimately comparable to that in England. Utility bills are large, luxury goods carry a massive import tax, and colonialism's legacy of an island with no sustaining agriculture means that almost all foodstuffs have to be brought in. A meal out in any restaurant will cost ten pounds a head, half a day's wages for many.

There are also far fewer jobs available than there are in Britain. Tourism's complete dominance as an industry means that the available labour is very unpredictable—only a certain amount of money comes in, and for any potential growth the island depends on the whims of the frustratingly fickle foreign holidaymaking market. By our conventional economic and industrial rationales there should be long queues for jobs all around the country, with people working all day to earn enough to climb up and out, into the US or Britain. Before I went I was certain this would be the case, that anyone who could leave the island would do as soon as they had means, and make serious cash elsewhere, but again this is disproven by almost everyone you talk to—the vast majority have left at some point in their lives, for schooling or employment, but almost all have subsequently returned, despite the greater money on offer elsewhere. It seems that the lure of the island is genuinely too strong for many to stay away, including those sufficiently educated or experienced to take on lots of better-paid work elsewhere. They have simply chosen the quality of life here over the career-bashing in London or New York. It was whimsically pointed out to me the distinction between the slogans of the US and Antigua, "Land of the Free" and "Land of Sea and Sun" respectively—"You wanna know the difference between our slogan and theirs?", he asked me. "The American one's a load of bullshit." And on the surface, it's difficult to argue with him. People return here in their droves because they quite literally can't take the pace of the mad struggle to work in Britain and the US.

Aside from the advantages of the climate, another central tenet of this attitude is the easiness of the inhabitants with regard to these essentials of food and accommodation. If you're in need, there'll always be a bed for the night, just as you'll be offered meals by people you've scarcely met, simply as a matter of course. Overhearing a politician on the radio speaking about relieving food shortages in Antigua, one local man from one of the poorest parts of the capital, St. John's, responded crossly: "Boy he chat shit, no man ever starve in Antigua." As much as anything else it strikes one that an endemic selfishness in Britain is a big reason why suggestions of idleness are met with scathing retorts. If somebody stays at your house back home, or takes endless meals with you, because they have little money, the immediate reaction is a reproach, a "you should really think about getting a job, shouldn't you?"

Obviously there are going to be limits to such an approach, but fundamentally its solution is, like so many solutions, a question of tolerance. In Antigua it is accepted that some people, and most people at one time or another, will not want to be enslaved in constant work. It is a choice that you are free to make, without being condemned by your peers. But in Britain, on the other hand, and even more so in the US, people are incredibly impatient with those that don't work. In some American companies taking a vacation, or certainly more than a week every year off, is seen as a lack of dedication and will hinder the development of your career. In Britain, even those with sufficient independent means to spend their whole lives not working, or working on a hobby, are met with resentment and suspicion. Those who inherit are treated almost as lower because of it, as if a lifetime of constant toil makes you an inherently better person. People are free to choose who they sleep with and where they shop, similarly in Antigua people are free to choose how much they work—if you happen for whatever reason not to need to work, then good for you.

Paradoxically this attitude means that people stay working for longer, which again brings unseen benefits. There is no retirement age, people work as they need to for as long as they need to. Because the labour is so much less intense and persistent, there is no case of people burning out as they approach fifty-five or sixty, waiting to be able to sit down in an easy chair and say: "I worked hard all my life for this," and settle down in expectation of falling off the twig, which

is essentially the system we have cultivated in Britain. Psychologically, stopping full-time employment is the signal for the commencement of old age and, ultimately, death, and in a time where medical advances mean that this really needn't be the case it is tragic. In Antigua it is common to see men of eighty or ninety, still with sculpted bodies, still doing the same fishing or running the same bars that they've done for endless years, and keeping up this activity, five or six hours a day, means that they too keep going. Rather than concentrating their leisure into twenty years after their working lives are done, they spread it evenly over a lifetime. It is far healthier and more natural than the society we have cultivated at home, where the old are shunted off in favour of the young, simply because youthful exuberance can be made to put in more hours.

Of course it's not all fantastic—there's a lot of poverty here, but the nature of its economy and its size mean that Antigua can never be rich enough to have the same per capita wealth as bigger countries. But though certain aspects—the inefficiency, for instance, could never be tolerated in Britain, the Antiguan work ethic still offers interesting and important lessons; most importantly remembering that we work to live. It's a fascinating phenomenon of Western holidaymaking that the most important parts to us are actually the processes of the trip—the planning, the packing, the leaving and then the memories, (hence our obsession with photographs). It's as if we've forgotten how to really relax. In Antigua they've never really learnt how to work. ◉

THE NON-CONFORMIST

Paul Hamilton on Dylan in the movies

Now the folk singer came from America
To sing at the Albert Hall
He sang his songs of protest
And fairer shares for all.
He sang how the poor were much too poor
And the rich too rich by far
Then he drove back to his penthouse
In his brand new Rolls Royce car.

Thus sang Benny Hill in a Sonny Bono twang over an "I Got You, Babe"-style folk-rock waltz, commemorating Bob Dylan's 1965 British tour that was more famously celebrated in D.A. Pennebaker's unapostrophised documentary *Don't Look Back*. Dylan, however, didn't need the warblings of a cherubic chortlemonger to bring home the contradictions inherent in singing songs of freedom in a shop-counter culture. Attempts by film makers, too, to address the matters of capitalism's crucial social inequality and class struggle can be interpreted variously as patronising, pretentious, woolly-brained or propagandist bilge produced by champagne socialists and lager liberals. Preston Sturges' *Sullivan's Travels* (1941) is a hilarious insight into the plight of the film director with the social conscience. He wants to live as a hobo amongst the dispossessed no-marks and discover what kind of film they wish to see: his lofty ideals descend like a concrete parachute when it transpires the proletariat are satisfied with Mickey Mouse, thank you

very much. (One wonders at Sturges' personal politics here. Was he being satirical, or was he a humbugging reactionary of the mindset that believed the leader who promised tuppence off a pint and tits in the paper would be guaranteed permanent power?)

There are remarkable similarities in political-extremist cinema, whatever stripe the film-makers' leanings are painted. D.W. Griffith's three-hour hymn to the Ku Klux Klan, *The Birth Of A Nation* (1915), is overwhelmingly epic in its scope, ambition and sentimentality. So too is Eisenstein's landmark telling of the Bolshevik uprising, *October 1917—Ten Days That Shook The World* ("Ha!" the neo-cons triumphantly roar, "Here we see Socialism at its worst. A ten day month? Already there are shortages!"). Griffith's negroes are looters and rapists, treacherous, Godless savages. Eisenstein's bourgeoisie are also broad caricatures—vain, insensitive, materialist. Both works are visceral, passionate, intensely powerful statements. Hitler, for one, understood how film can ignite the powderkegs of the populace and swayed public opinion with programmes of anti-Semitism and endorsed Leni Reifenstahl's decidedly more artful studies of the Aryan ideal. For all their undisputed creative brilliance, however, *October 1917* and *The Birth Of The Nation* remain, at their core, subtle-as-a-flying-sledgehammer pieces of overt flagwaving. Pier Paolo Pasolini,

BOB DYLAN IN 'RENALDO AND CLARA' (1978): MASKED AND UBIQUITOUS

the gay Marxist Italian poet, intellectual heavyweight and director, went totally overboard with his last film *Salo (120 Days Of Sodom)* (1975). His supposed allegory of fascism was a vile, relentlessly puke-inducing degradation-fest, where naked young men and women are buggered and tortured by a committee of obese, jaded old men. Oh, how poetic, how true. "Ah, you see how clever Pasolini is here," an earnest cineaste apologist would gush, "for whereas in real life the working classes metaphorically eat shit and die, here they literally *are* forced to eat shit."

When the opportunities arose, Bob Dylan eagerly made films of a specifically non-linear nature, resisting the urge to nail his true colours to a post. His three works—*Eat The Document* (directed with Howard Alk, 1967), *Renaldo And Clara* (again with Alk, 1977) and *Masked And Anonymous* (2003, written by Dylan and its director Larry Charles)—eschew the established rules of film-making. The narratives are elusive, dreamlike; characters are enigmatic; time is inconstant, forever flipping forwards and back again. Rather than make a Protest Film About An Issue, Dylan's films are protests against film-

making itself. *Eat The Document* is his reaction to Pennebaker's excellent *Don't Look Back*. Its fly-on-the-wall traditional documentary style was probably too formal for Dylan's taste—too revealing, perhaps. *DLB* concentrated on how Dylan is perceived by outsiders—agents, fans, journalists—and how Dylan deals with them. With ...*Document*, Dylan and Alk reverse the view and show what the eye of the hurricane sees. ...*Document* is an attempt to construct a film in the same way Dylan composes a song, only instead of lyrics setting scenes and introducing thumbnail sketch characters (such as *Little Boy Lost, The Night Watchman, Louise, The Peddler* and *The Jelly-Faced Women* of *Visions of Johanna*), and rhythm and melody, guitar lines and keyboard colours, he uses snippets of film, fragments of dialogue. The result is a frustration because our expectations are constantly dashed. Ecstatic live footage is cut after a minute, yet boring off-duty skits, such as piano player Richard Manuel offering a young man some trinkets for his girlfriend, seem to drag eternally. This is perhaps Dylan's statement on the reality of the pop star's lot—fragmented, confused, inconclusive.

Remembrance Of Things, Pissed would be an appropriate subtitle.

Visual leitmotifs are abundant in *...Document*: the steam train tearing through the countryside; the flat-capped boss-eyed bloke staring into the camera; the wanly smiling blond woman sitting, watching and waiting; the crush of fans at a venue; red-rimmed eyes of the musicians hiding behind hipster shades. There's a memorable cameo by a sandwich man who stands near Dylan when he's in a crowd watching a display of police dog skills. The board on his chest reads IT IS APPOINTED UNTO MEN ONCE TO DIE. When he turns away we see AFTER DEATH THE JUDGEMENT emblazoned on his back board. (It's almost a lyric from Dylan's later born-again phase repertoire.) The soundtrack is cleverly arranged. Organist Garth Hudson's soundcheck doodles segues seamlessly into a street scene of military bagpipers. Snatches of Dylan dialogue emerge: "I'm sorry for everything I've done... and hope to remedy it soon," he states baldly. He is more emphatic when a journo asks him why he doesn't sing protest songs anymore. "All I *do* is protest," Bob protests. There's a very shaky rendition of "I Still Miss Someone" backstage with Dylan obliviously playing the wrong tune on a piano rested on by a shockingly thin Johnny Cash. The other celebrity cameo is John Lennon, suited, shaded and paranoid, riding with Bob in the back of a car chauffeured by Brian Jones of The Rolling Stones' man, Tom Keylock. Both spokesmen for their generation are wrecked—Dylan biliously stoned, Lennon merely marbled. Lennon mocks Dylan's fragile condition with a TV ad voice-over: "Do you suffer from sore eyes, groovy forehead or curly? TAKE ZIMDON!" As they speed through the dawn rainy London streets, Bob's hungover groans are met with scant sympathy: "Permission to land,

TONY GAUNIER AND BOB DYLAN IN 'MASKED AND ANONYMOUS', 2003: THE RECORD SHOWS HE TOOK BLOWS

Tom," drawls John. Outside the Fellini-like circus are the chorus of fans after the tent's been pulled down: "Rubbish!... Absolutely fantastic... Terrible... Yeah, 'sgreat, man... It were a bloody disgrace. He wants shooting. He's a traitor!"

The application of songwriting modes to film-making is only a partial success, even after repeated viewings. *Eat the Document* is Dylan murmuring to himself, not singing to the people. In songs like "A Hard Rain's A-Gonna Fall", "Desolation Row" and "Chimes Of Freedom", Dylan can take chains of disparate images and bind them to a majestic conclusion. The riddles, epigrams, in-jokes that work as lyrics when transposed to the film medium are left hanging in the air or flat on the floor. "Eat The Document" refuses to add up, its strands unresolved, which may be Dylan and Alk's perverse intention ("There's no success like failure and failure's no success at all," as Bob gnomically sang in "Love Minus Zero/No Limit"), but to even the most ardent Bob head (who, after all, are the only ones who would be interested in it), it's sadly unsatisfactory. Dylan withdrew it from public release, preferring to let the legend of it prosper.

Bob Dylan is wearing a Richard Nixon mask and singing about when he paints his masterpiece, which means he's on his Rolling Thunder Revue tour of late '75 and we're watching Renaldo And Clara in a cinema in 1978 or at home with a bootleg videotape of it right about now. Lasting a few minutes shy of four hours—about the same length as a Bollywood trailer—Dylan and Alk have, once again, neglected silly, bourgeois things like drama, plot development, character studies. This time, rather than cut the film together "musically", they have opted for a more painterly sensibility. A colour or object that appears at the end of one scene will be seen at the beginning of the next. Hats and flowers predominate; Dylan saw a flower-decorated hat as a metaphor for love: "a travelling vagina" was his term for it. Strangely enough, although Renaldo And Clara has so much in its disfavour—long scenes are improvised by non-actors (band members, genial loon Allen Ginsberg, even Bob's sassy street apple wife Sara), the total incomprehension of what the fuck is supposed to be going on—it works beautifully. The time flies by, your subconscious enjoying having to make the associational links. It's a primitive interactive game. Dylan, such an exciting, visceral, magnetic onstage performer, is a negligible presence in the dramatic scenes. He fails to open up. He won't open his mouth for fear that his feet end up in it. (Just like Frank Zappa in his extraordinary 200 Motels.)

The half-baked symbolism aside, Renaldo And Clara contains the best-shot footage of any live band ever. Dylan was accused by Pauline Kael of narcissism and megalomania for the abundance of full-screen facial close-ups. Regarding their film in terms of moving paintings, Dylan and Alk were absolutely right to concentrate on the face (and not solely Dylan's) since art is primarily concerned with portraiture. With the concert footage, they ignore the usual cliches of cameras swooping over the cheering masses (yer Glastonbury pan) and go right to the source of the energy—the faces and the hands of the musicians. The rollicking, gonzoid performance of "Isis" is revelatory in its simplicity. Shot principally with one camera, there are two and a half minutes of Dylan passionately hollering in whiteface make-up (the spectre of minstrelsy would be conjured up again in "Masked and Anonymous", as indeed is the moustache he draws on his face in 'Eat The Document') before we cut to a different angle. For the songs alone, Renaldo And Clara is a must-see. The unresolved dramas, rendered in cut-up and collaged form, is a mindgame but not the alienating one of Eat The Document. Renaldo And Clara was a critical hit in Britain and Europe, enjoying multi-month runs at arthouse cinemas. In America, of course, it was lambasted and Dylan was "encouraged" to cut his celluloid canvas to a more palatable two hours. He shouldn't have capitulated. Far better had he added another couple of hours.

In the 25 years that divide Renaldo And Clara and Masked And Anonymous, Bob Dylan underwent significant changes. He found Jesus and lost his audience. He became evermore paranoid in maintaining his privacy, and this compulsion for zipped lips extended even to his memoirs. His first volume of autobiography, Chronicles, was a beguiling, charming, slippery work. He mentions his wife in the chapter centred on 1970—we know it's Sara but she is never named. The wife referred to in the "Oh Mercy" section is also unidentified. One has to consult another

BOB DYLAN IN MASKED AND ANONYMOUS, 2003

biography of Dylan to establish that her name is Carolyn Dennis. Mischievous as ever, Dylan provokes more questions than answers, and his book could be a protest against confessionals. He also underwent a number of crises in confidence about his songwriting, suffering blocks that lasted years, the longest being from 1991 to 1997. Whilst he had invariably utilized an ancient blues lyric or two in the past and somehow given them a fresh, humorous twist, it seems that the modern Dylan is shaping entire songs from other, obscure sources. The texts of *Love And Theft* (2001) and *Modern Times* (2006) are stacked with quotes from blues and country obscurities, a biography of a Japanese yakuza, American civil war poets, Frank Sinatra standards, movie dialogue, a quote from a Van Dyke Parks interview. Nothing scandalous or shocking, you might think. Songwriters take their inspiration from anything and anyone. Like Warhol and the 60s Pop Artists, they take whatever is around and transform it into Art. The Beatles' "Being For The Benefit Of Mr Kite" is composed entirely from an Edwardian circus poster, and their "Golden Slumbers"

was a direct copy of a nursery rhyme by playwright Thomas Dekker, a contemporary of Shakespeare. Dialogue from Orson Welles' *Citizen Kan* make up the entire lyrics for The White Stripes' "The Union Forever". Radiohead have slipped in quotes from the Anthony Clare and Spike Milligan book, *Depression And How To Survive It*. So it goes, but no-one has taken it to Dylan's extent. He is trying to eradicate the (ridiculous, impossible) mantle of Spokesman For A Generation, and be Mr No Comment. In Terry Gilliam's *Brazil* (1985) Robert De Niro—who had spent his few previous scenes hidden under a balaclava and thick glasses—reveals his face for a moment and is then suddenly caught in a typhoon of newspapers that wrap themselves around him, obscuring him totally. He collapses on the street, flailing pathetically. Jonathan Pryce comes to his aid, frantically pulling the newsheets away. When he has done so, he finds De Niro has disappeared. It's like that with Dylan now. He's become like one of his own creations, the Preacher in "Stuck Inside Of Mobile" who has "twenty pounds of headlines stapled to his chest". If all his cryptic references were stripped from him, what would he say? The songs on his two recent records sound funky and fun, but they don't mean an awful lot. Is he pathologically shy of making The Big Statement or The Personal Revelation? Is there anything that need be said, anyway? Dylan had been almost permanently on tour duty since 1988. Had he become like Welles' sailor in *The Lady From Shanghai* (1947) who had been around the world so often he ended up knowing nothing about it? Well, there was plenty to be said in *Masked And Anonymous*, but, naturally, it had be said elliptically, elusively, allusively. This time the directing duties were handled by Larry Charles (the helmsman of *Borat: Cultural Learnings Of America For Make Benefit*

Glorious Nation Of Kazakhstan, a Stupid's Arrow hitting the bull's eye of Occidental idiocy) and there was even a semblance of a plot line.

A Third World America is in the final throes of a civil war. Its elderly libertarian President is nearing death. His neo-con son lurks in the wings, awaiting the opportunity to seize power. To raise funds for war victims, the government-controlled TV station propose a rock'n'roll benefit concert. All the big names have refused, sensing the show to be a propaganda exercise for dubious political ends. The TV producers' last resort is Jack Fate (guess who?), a pivotal Sixties icon now languishing in gaol...

S hot in less than three weeks on location in the parts of Los Angeles that the tourists never see, Masked And Anonymous is as cryptic and open, as heart-warming and spine-chilling, as the best of Bob Dylan's songs. The only trouble is this isn't a song—although its genesis was a pile of discarded lyrics for Dylan's Love And Theft album, which Dylan and Charles assembled in a William Burroughs cut-up fashion (Burroughs is referenced on a hotel lobby noticeboard as "Dr Benway—Psychiatrist").Dylan and Charles—screenwriting as Sergei Petrov and Rene Fontaine—have concocted a satiric fable, firing a blunderbuss at both the post-Live Aid neutering of protest music and the hippy idealistic notion that only music can stop wars and change the world, maaaaaaan (Dylan still sitting comfortably on the fence). Other targets include the worship of false idols, treacherous politicians, philanthropic hypocrites—yer standard Dylan obsessional stash, of course.

Critics were predictably hostile to Masked And Anonymous, dismissing it as a curate's egg for the incurable Zimmophile, a plotless, pretentious yawnfest for the uninitiated. Bollocks to those windbag shitpots. Bob Dylan is hilariously eccentric In his portrayal of Jack Fate. Not for him the acutely-observed performance of, say, Gwyneth Paltrow in Shallow Hal, where her walking-stick frame miraculously conveyed the gait and discomfort of a morbidly obese woman. Nope, none of that. Even more than Renaldo And Clara, Bob consummately fails to respond or emote to anything or anyone, not even Jeff Bridges' bellowing in-yer-face Dylan-dress-alike disillusioned veteran rock hack. Dylan's Chauncey Gardiner in a cowboy hat, he's Kasper Hauser in a Vincent Price 'tache. It's a perverse performance—anti-acting, really. Jack Fate's last words before the credits roll ("I stopped trying to figure everything out a long time ago") are profoundly moving. One feels crushed that Dylan feels this way, that he has lost his curiosity and sense of wonder, that he has resigned from active service. He says it, though, with a rare kind of happiness, a Zen-blissed acceptance of his lot. And, as with Renaldo And Clara, perhaps Masked And Anonymous is Jack Fate's dream and he is simply sleepwalking through it, like Lewis Carroll's Alice. Certainly, the film has a fractured dream-like logic and flow to it. It reads like a kicked jigsaw, and, like Alice In Wonderland, there are plenty of potty cameos—Val Kilmer's parody of Brando in Apocalypse Now is succulently hammy. Jack Fate only breaks out of his somnambulism when he sings in that shredded, razors'n'rum voice, Larry Charles capturing the performances in single fish-eye lens extreme close-ups.

Masked And Anonymous—with its underlying Catch-22 menace and Natural Born Killers-like schizo moodswings and roundabouts—is, whether he likes it or not, an idiosyncratic revelation of the bats in Bob Dylan's hat. Long may they keep flapping. 🌀

53 Sloane Square, London, SW1X 8AX
Tel: 0207.259.9566.

207 Westbourne Grove, London, W11 2SF
Tel: 0207.731.7490.

33 Amwell Street, London, EC1 1UR
Tel: 0207.833.2367.

www.emmahope.co.uk

Fourteen Years, 38 Back Issues

1: August '93
SOLD OUT
Dr Johnson
Terence McKenna

2: Nov-Dec '93
SOLD OUT
Homer Simpson
Will Self

3: Jan-Feb '94
£8.00
Bertrand Russell
Charles Handy

4: April-May '94
SOLD OUT
Kurt Cobain
Matt Black

5: July-Aug '94
SOLD OUT
Douglad Coupland
Jerome K. Jerome

6: Sept-Oct '94
SOLD OUT
Easy Listening
Richard Linklater

7: Dec-Jan '95
SOLD OUT
Sleep
Gilbert Shelton

8: Feb-Mar '95
SOLD OUT
Jeffrey Bernard
Robert Newman

9: May-June '95
SOLD OUT
Suzanne Moore
Positive Drinking

10: July-Aug '95
SOLD OUT
Damian Hirst
Will Self

11: Sept-Oct '95
£4.00
Keith Allen
Dole Life

12: Nov-Dec '95
£4.00
Bruce Robinson
All Night Garages

TO ORDER YOUR BACK ISSUES:

Go to www.idler.co.uk or write to The Idler, P.O Box 280, Barnstaple, EX31 4WX. You must include P&P cost as follows: **P&P:** Issues 1-24: 50p per issue. Issues 25-38: £2 per issue. For European Community, add 50%. For Rest of World, add 100%

13: Jan-Feb '96
SOLD OUT
Stan Lee
Life As A Kid

14: Mar-Apr '96
£4.00
Bruce Reynolds
Will Self

14: May-June '96
SOLD OUT
Hashish Killers
Alex Chilton

16: Aug-Sept '96
SOLD OUT
John Michel
World Poker

17: Nov-Dec '96
SOLD OUT
John Cooper Clarke
Cary Grant

18: Spring '97
SOLD OUT
Thomas Pynchon
Ivan Illich

19: Summer '97
£4.00
Psychography
Henry Miller

20: Winter '97
SOLD OUT
Howard Marks
Kenny Kramer

21: Feb-March '98
SOLD OUT
The Gambler
Bez

22: April-May '98
SOLD OUT
Alan Moore
Alex james

23: June-July '98
SOLD OUT
Summer special
Tim Roth

24: Aug-Sept '98
SOLD OUT
Summer special
Tim Roth

MAN'S RUIN
25: Winter 1999
£15
The first book-format Idler, featuring Louis Theroux's Sick Notes, Will Self, Howard Marks, Adam and Joe and Ken Kesey

PARADISE
26: Summer 2000
£5
Jonathan Coe meets David Nobbs, Nicholas Blincoe on Sherlock Holmes, Tiki Special, Iain Sinclair on the London Eye

THE FOOL
27: Winter 2000
£5
Village Idiots, Arthur Smith's diary, The Big Quit, James Jarvis's World of Pain, John Lloyd

RETREAT
28: Summer 2001
£10
Louis Theroux meets Bill Oddie, Jonathan Ross meets Alan Moore, Alex James meets Patrick Moore plus Andrew Loog Oldham

HELL
29: Winter 2001
£10
Crass Founder Penny Rimbaud, Crap Jobs Special, Boredom Section, new fiction from Niall Griffiths, Mark Manning, Billy Childish

LOVE
30: Summer 2002
SOLD OUT
Louis Theroux meets Colin Wilson, Johnny Ball on Descartes, Crap Towns, Devon Retreat, Chris Yates interview, Marchesa Casati

REVOLUTION
31: Winter 2002
£10
Dave Stuart, Black Panthers, Saint Monday, Allotments, Riots, Introducing the Practical Idler section

ANNIVERSARY
32: Winter 2003
£10
Damian Hirst on why cunts sell shit to fools, Marc Bolan, the pleasures of the top deck, Walt Whitman, happines

TO ORDER GO TO WWW.IDLER.CO.UK

LADIES OF LEISURE
33: Spring 2004
£10
Clare Pollard is sick of
shopping; Girls on bass; the wit
and wisdom of Quentin Crisp;
Barbara Ehrenreich

THE FOOD ISSUE
34: Winter 2004
£10
Joan Bakewell on life as a
freelancer; Bill Drummond's
soup adventure; The Giro
Playboy; Falconry; why
supermarkets are evil and
Jerome K Jerome

WAR ON WORK
35: Spring 2005
£10
Keith Allen's A to Z of life; Raoul
Vaneigem interview; Jeremy
Deller's Folk Art; Dan Kieran's
Seven Steps To The Idle Life;
Chris Donald, Peter Doherty
and more Crap Jobs

**YOUR MONEY
OR YOUR LIFE**
36: Winter 2005
£10
Mutoid Waste Company;
Edward Chancellor on credit,
Penny Rimbaud; Jay Griffiths; A
Hitch Hikers Guide; The Guilds;
Chris Donald

CHILDISH THINGS
37: Spring 2005
£10
Childcare for the Lazy; Michael
Palin, Bertrand Russell; Free
Range Education; Running
Away to Join the Circus

THE GREEN MAN
38: WINTER 2006
£10.99
Stephan Harding on why
doing less is the way forward;
Richard Benson tries to sow a
meadow; in conversation with
Jamie Reid; John Michell on
Cobbett; plus ukulele special

TO ORDER GO TO WWW.IDLER.CO.UK

THE VIEW FROM THE SOFA

If you want to be radical, says Greg Rowland, just say nothing

Moaning, protesting, whining, righteous hand-wringing or creating situationalist moments to attempt the destabilisation of symbolic norms is a whole lotta fun. It's a pleasant leisure activity for the radical bourgeoisie, and generally harms nobody. Of course it's unlikely to change anything, except perhaps in the most subtle and incremental ways. Our culture actively encourages us to rebel. It's part of the same expression of individuality that makes us consumers.

Please feel free to shout to shout, protest and rebel to your heart's content, because whatever you do will be absorbed into the economic mainframe. It's like the old TSB slogan. Capitalism is the ideology that likes to say "Yes". By the very act of considering yourself important enough to have an individual opinion you've already bought into the culture that supports Western liberalism and capital.

So every time you buy anything, whether it's a tube of Smarties or a Bentley, you're part of the system. This applies doubly to certain flavour variants of Walker's "Sensations", for reasons that I am not at liberty to disclose at this present time.

The stupid alternative articulation of "No" is to get down with some crazy theological totalitarianism and blow yourself up in public. This is not a course of action I would recommend. It's terribly impolite to murder and maim people without their express permission beforehand.

Let's therefore address the perennial revolutionary question posed by Lenin: what is to be done? First we have to rid ourselves of the Narcissus Complex that promotes us to rebel. Whether you're a good old-fashioned activist or a theocratic nutcase I suggest you radically decentre yourself. Stop trying to impress people with your me-me-me commitment. Stop being the hero of your own life narrative. Become a supporting player: become he who is merely Mr Chekhov rather than he who wishes to be Captain Kirk.

Once you have rid yourself of the impression that you or any of your ideas have any significance whatsoever, the truly radical opportunity gently taps you on the shoulder. March with placards that demonstrate your lack of importance —"Please don't look at me" or "My opinions will only be validated if somehow consistent with the vagaries of global capitalism". And, perhaps, in two or three hundred years something will imperceptibly change for the better. ◉